MEGATON MORNINGS

BY

CHARLES HALL

OWL PRESS

Published by Owl Press, P.O Box 315 Downton, Salisbury, Wiltshire. SP5 3YE. 1993
Printed in the UK by BPCC Wheatons Ltd, Exeter.

British Library Cataloguing - in - Publication data. A catalogue record for this book is available from the British Library.

Publisher's ISBN: 1 898052 01 8

AUTHOR'S NOTE

The events described in this story are true, although the names of the men involved have been changed. Memory was aided by reference to daily letters sent home from Christmas Island during the period from November 1961 to November 1962.

When British servicemen were observing nuclear tests in the Pacific during the 1950s, the Prime Minister at that time, Sir Anthony Eden, was warned they risked lingering death from cancer. His response, was reported to have been, 'A pity, but we cannot help it.'

Charles Hall

ACKNOWLEDGEMENTS

A very special thanks to my wife Jacqueline for her deep involvement in the creation of this book.

My thanks to author Garry Kilworth for his advice and friendly encouragement, which kept us on course for its completion.

Thanks also to Clelland Barrie, fellow Christmas Island veteran for his tireless efforts to keep additional information flowing in our direction and for confirming some of the details contained in this story.

For Corinne, John and Peter

'Dark with excessive bright.'

Milton. Paradise Lost.

CHAPTER ONE

Paradise lost

The sound scratched at my brain and made me stir reluctantly. Patches of sweat clung around my neck and lay on my chest. An all-consuming lethargy anchored me to the narrow bed. Even before heavy eyelids flickered slowly open, I was aware of the hot greyness of the tropical morning which surrounded me with its clammy presence.

The sound intruded once more, 'This is Mahatma. This is Mahatma. D minus ten minutes. D minus ten minutes.'

I turned over. A shaft of diffused light from the lamp outside the billet outlined the lifeless shapes of my four companions. They were not yet stirring.

I rolled onto my back again, closed my eyes and lay still. Thoughts struggled to surface as the mind hovered between waking and sleep. D minus ten minutes, a few minutes to detonation. It must be nearly six-thirty in the morning, an hour before dawn.

I lay and waited. The tannoy outside the window, the source of the tormenting sound, continued to bark out at intervals. Then it stopped abruptly.

At that moment, through closed eyes, the darkness suddenly became patterned with blood red. I did not move. I did not open my eyes. I knew already what it would be like outside; I had seen it too many times before. In seconds, the harsh flash of light always expanded from blinding speck to monstrous ball of violent white. The island moved from night to instant day. The Pacific

7

waters surrounding the island lapped uneasily as they bathed in the light from a man made sun. They lay cowed, licked by unnatural energy which radiated from above, as from the wing of some death angel covering the sky. I wanted no more part of it. It was, after all, the ultimate horror.

My body tensed involuntarily. The twenty-fifth hydrogen bomb had just been detonated and it was the last one for me. I forced tensed muscles to relax, to relax before the onslaught of sound and movement which came with the inevitable and deafening crack of earth shattering blast. It would be finished soon. As the seconds ticked away, the question that always came to mind insisted on being asked again. 'What the hell am I doing here?'

Pacific paradise, that is what the Sergeant had called it. But then, that was in England and he had never been to the island.

I was amongst the last to be conscripted when the Royal Air Force dragged me into its all powerful embrace.

Strangely enough, I was not overawed by what fate had presented and, in a moment of weird aberration, I signed away an extra three years of freedom and became a regular at the age of twenty. Not only did I expect an interesting overseas posting but looked forward to it with enthusiastic optimism and some excitement. What seemed like exotic territories, such as Singapore and Hong Kong, together with many other attractive outposts, beckoned temptingly.

In fact 'join Her Majesty's Service and see the world' seemed a good proposition then. There were many overseas postings to which I could also take Jacqueline. Presented with a form for choice, I ticked the 'ACCOMPANIED POSTINGS' box and sat back thinking life was very sweet, convinced that the world lay before us. It was true that the trade of wireless operator attracted the most remote and desolate places on Earth but there were plenty of single men who wanted those postings.

Trusting and confident, one year into my service days and now with a baby daughter as well as a wife, I bypassed the notice-board. This displayed station routine orders and its regimented lists were updated regularly. They gave information about station activities, rosters for parade or guard duty, promotions and punishments as well as overseas postings. It was an offence not to read the notices daily, but there was always an avid notice-board reader who would be eager to inform anything of interest to anybody. One of the world's natural organizers was always around.

It was one such helpful, conscientious individual, a skinny Leading Aircraftman (LAC), who informed me of my new overseas posting when, one day, I happily entered the communications' centre. He stood up to aggressive questioning. He was unnervingly positive, absolutely sure. Disbelief shot through me. This was one place I had not thought of. I moved rapidly, skidding out of the room and broke into a run down the corridor. Then my brain caught up with my legs and sent them back to the communications' centre.

'Where's the bloody board?' I demanded belligerently.

The composed LAC looked slowly up and gave dispassionate directions. His tone made it clear that his role was not to care, only to inform. I charged down the narrow passages again. I came to the board and leaned against it trying to regain breath, at the same time scanning the mass of printed matter. Panic gradually gave way to feelings of frustration and a sense of futility. There it was, 'SAC Hall, posting: Christmas Island, November 1961, day to be confirmed later.' This was certainly one place I had not thought of.

After signing off duty at midday, I hurried over to the administration office. An age passed waiting at the end of a short queue to see the Sergeant in charge. Eventually my turn came.

'Christmas Island, Sarge? Unaccompanied posting? There must be some mistake?'

A few minutes passed while the Sergeant sifted through some papers. He was still looking down as his reply came back.

'There is no mistake. That is the posting allocated to you.'

He looked up, his eyes a steady gaze beneath unflickering lids; the strong square look of those in control.

'Pacific paradise,' he said convincingly, before he looked down again, adding quickly, 'it's only a year anyway.'

A year, a whole year! My worst fears were realized. Christmas Island; from what I knew a coral rock, a rock surrounded by sea, miles from anywhere. Reminiscent of Devil's Island, it seemed more like a prison sentence than an opportunity to see the world. Also, as nobody on this RAF station had been there, it was impossible to gather any reliable information about the place. There was a little fourth and fifth hand speculation that atom bombs had been tested there, but it was generally agreed that it was 'a pisshole of a posting'.

If I could have made time stand still in the weeks that followed, I would have done. But somehow the days and nights slipped by. Time did what it had to do; it stopped for nobody anywhere and certainly not for us. The evening came when I faced Jacky on the railway station platform not knowing how to say goodbye. There was no need to say much; the grey rain, drizzling jagged curtains around us, spoke for Jacky and me.

England is well suited for sad departures. Rain was meeting damp mist from the Essex Thames Estuary river creeks which stretched in veins across the marshland lying beyond the railway station. The place wept quietly in the dusk and the dull orange street lamps blinked through a haze of wet monochrome. Survival was bred into both of us. We were two, among many, of a generation born in war who knew it was lucky to survive; our fathers had come home from prisoner-of-war camps and service overseas.

The black shape of the steam train loomed up and hissed its clumsy way into Benfleet station.

'Look after my baby,' I said as I bent to kiss her.

'You mean your babies,' she corrected softly; her words hardly audible against the sound of the rain on the umbrella held over us. She was certain now that we were to have another child.

Along the station, carriage doors slammed and whistles screeched. Bursts of steam screamed wildly as the train lurched forward. How many times, for how many people this scene? Leaning from the carriage window to touch as long as possible, the train a jailor who breaks lovers from each other.

So, like all true warriors and heroes I went from her, she who is supposed to stand and wait, to face a journey to the other side of the world. I was leaving paradise behind in England and in the rain. So what was this sunny island, lying in the middle of nowhere, in the shadow of the atom bomb?

CHAPTER TWO

Preparations

Waiting at the informal airport lounge were some men with their wives and children, including some babies in carrycots. I thought of Jacky and the baby I would not see for a year and of the one that would be born while I was away. These men had been allowed home to collect their families so that they could travel together on accompanied postings. Everyone was dressed in civilian clothing as was customary when travelling on non-military aircraft. The whole scene resembled a package holiday; cases and kit bags were scattered about and large Singapore labels flapped from their handles.

I had spent the previous 24 hours or so being kitted out at RAF Gloucester along with many other servicemen en route to the Near East and Far East. Here, men were led around in batches of about twenty and groups were constantly on the move between various rooms, buildings and areas.

'Shorts for the use of: three pairs,' the civilian storekeeper had chanted in standard Forces' jargon.

'Khaki trousers for the use of: three pairs.'

Civilians were the most dictatorial and unbending of storekeepers. They were beyond the control of military discipline and even an officer could not order them to issue anything from their stores without proper documentation. They seemed to see themselves as having sole power and control. This was a trait that we quickly turned to our advantage and approached them accordingly.

'I don't suppose it's possible for you to issue me with an extra pair of sunglasses is it? I mean I don't want to get you into any trouble.'

The feigned innocent concern invariably conjured up the desired response, 'I'm in charge here. It's up to me what I give out. Here you are son.' And the spare items would be slapped firmly down on the long counter in front of us.

My feelings of satisfaction at the ability to manipulate storekeepers had turned to smugness when asked to produce current vaccination and inoculation certificates. I had already suffered these at the previous station and was in no mood to feel sorry for anyone. I even began to feel uncharacteristically sadistic as the unfortunate queue of mixed shapes and sizes shuffled an uneven, apprehensive way to meet with protection against yellow fever, typhoid and tetanus, smallpox and so on. With this number of men, the needles were discarded only when they became so blunt that they failed to penetrate the next arm reluctantly offered. The degree of discomfort built up in waves, from fresh needle to battered discard.

Then, after a thorough medical had pronounced a number of us fit for overseas duty, we filed into a large hall to hear a long lecture about the perils of foreign lands. Some of the people present gave the impression that they already knew these perils only too well; if a knife or bullet did not get you, venereal disease or snake bites would. Someone in the row directly behind muttered something about just keeping your head down and your pants up. However, the dangers droned on for a considerable time, until I was startled out of a semi-dazed state by the snoring of the man next to me. This jolt back into full consciousness coincided with question and answer time. There were no questions.

The lecturer had seemed slightly disconcerted by this lack of concern but we were not. It had meant that we could leave ten minutes early and find a position at the front of the queue at the airmen's mess, now prepared for the worse the world had to offer.

I met nobody, nor had I met anybody during the previous day or evening who would be sharing the same destination as myself. I had been unperturbed by this; the fact that I was going had seemed enough to occupy the mind. But now I felt lonely among the crowds of chattering strangers at the airport, although the atmosphere was cordial enough.

Then on this cold, wet, windy evening, Tuesday 14 November, I strode across the tarmac to the waiting British United Airways Britannia turbo-prop aircraft. With cine-camera slung over shoulder and boarding-pass in hand, I ascended the short flight of steps and entered the plane. A smiling stewardess gave directions to a seat next to one of the giant Bristol Proteus engines on the port side of the aircraft. I sat down and shivered slightly with cold or nervous tension. Large blobs of rain splattered against the outside of the window as I watched the reflections of passengers moving to their seats.

The sound of somebody slumping into the next seat interrupted any imminent feelings of depression.

'Hello, I'm Brian,' my neighbour volunteered.

'Chas. Where are you going?'

'Hickam,' he replied. He sounded extremely pleased with himself.

'Never heard of it. Where is it?'

'Hawaii.' He was looking even more self-satisfied. 'And you?'

'Christmas Island.' Somehow it did not sound as romantic as Hawaii.

He was Welsh, the same build as myself, about 5ft 11in with a medium frame. Underneath dark wavy hair curled tighter by damp from the rain, he had a naturally good-natured face which added to his air of happy self-congratulation. We soon discovered that we were both in the same trade. The fact that he could also operate a teleprinter made his posting to Hawaii possible and, for the first time, I regretted having turned down the extra twelve week course.

Doors firmly closed and seat belts fastened, the engines began to turn, quickly gathering speed to an almost deafening pitch. The plane shook and began to inch forward.

'Flown before Brian?'

'No, great isn't it?' He grinned widely. The Welsh accent in his voice made him seem excited and enthusiastic. I did not answer. The great aircraft lumbered to the edge of the runway.

'We're airborne,' Brian stated dramatically. It seemed that to add to the occasion the Welsh like to put most things into words.

'You might be, but the plane's still taxiing,' I replied peering out of the window. His youthful enthusiasm was infectious and I tried to sound matter of fact although I too had never flown before.

The plane began to accelerate down the runway, pulsing and swaying, until it took off into the black void of the night.

CHAPTER THREE

The journey

The journey was long. There were short refuelling stops, where we felt the warm nights of Istanbul and Bombay, but otherwise sleep came and went as we cat-napped our way to Singapore.

It was four o' clock in the morning, when we left the aircraft but the air felt hot and sticky. Blue, Royal Air Force, single-decker buses waited in line outside the terminal building and gave a clear indication that, at last, there was to be some respite from air travel. We were to spend a few days in transit accommodation at RAF Changi before travelling on to final destinations.

Singapore was quick to absorb and fascinate. On the road to Changi camp the bus headlamps stabbed into lush, green-polished undergrowth and occasionally outlined the shape of palm trees. Monkeys chattered as they leapt and somersaulted in trees surrounding the base and everyone was impatient to see more of these strange surroundings.

Information was exchanged rapidly when the bus first arrived at the camp. Almost immediately, an airman who came from my home town walked over to greet us and invited me to join him and his friends for a swim that morning. Impatience to see more and the hotness of the day compelled me to agree readily; it was a decision that I was to regret bitterly.

The beach at Changi was deserted at ten o'clock in the morning and the empty sand stretched out in front of a sea that sparkled and glittered invitingly in the early sun. We made our way down to the water and the sand felt hot on the soles of the feet. We plunged into a sea that felt like a lukewarm bath which was cool and refreshing compared to the heavy humidity of the beach.

The airman and his friends had been in Singapore for some months and were sporting fine tans. Well aware that it took time to build up such a tan, and being fair skinned as well as winter pale, I decided to leave them after about an hour. We arranged to meet later that evening and I left them on the beach lying bronzed and motionless under the sun.

Afternoon found me gazing apprehensively at red skin in the mirror, very red skin. By the time the evening meal was over, it was clear that the sun had stayed with me; it felt as though flames were trying to engulf my body. I decided not to go out. Cloistered in the room, lying on top of the bed, I tried to read but found concentration impossible.

Unable to sleep, the night that followed seemed endless. It brought little comfort to stare at the ceiling and watch the bright green chit-chat lizards catching flies. Even so, hours were spent gazing at these creatures, about four inches in length, their movements almost unnoticeable as they inched carefully and craftily towards their prey. The huge ceiling fans whirred unceasingly but did little to cool the burning red skin. Careless sunburn was interpreted as a self-inflicted injury and desperate thoughts of obtaining medication from the sick bay were quashed.

During this long, long night I saw a bed bug for the first time. It was a revolting little creature. It stained the white sheet with a red blot as I squashed its blood-filled body between finger and thumb.

When, at last, the night ended, I eased myself out of bed and got dressed slowly. A tired, red and sore face glared unhappily from the mirror and stated that washing and shaving were out of the question.

Brian's eyes opened in exaggerated horror when he saw the same face later that morning.

'You've got it bad! Does it hurt?' he taunted.

He started to sing tunefully *Mad Dogs and Englishmen go out in the Midday Sun*. He knew some of the words of the song but trailed off, after a few lines, stating that he was glad he was not English if they all ended up looking like that.

'You'll never do well at the Eisteddfod with a voice like yours,' I countered. But the curiosity to see Singapore was stronger than the pain of sunburn and we set off to see the sights, keeping out of the sun, dodging in and out of the shade. The day turned out to be one of noisy streets and frantic movement; hours caught in a human sized ant's nest.

It was market time in Changi Village; a spider's web of shops and stalls formed an Aladdin's cave around the main street. We were continually accosted by vendors trying to sell their goods which were open to barter. The more resistant the customer, the more excited and animated they became. Their rapid, whining speech reached fever pitch as they feigned desperation at the lack of a sale. By the time that we got out of the market we were loaded with goods costing a fraction of the UK price and which, like musical cigarette lighters, fascinated our utilitarian moulded minds.

Changi, in its turn, was a haven of peace compared to the city of Singapore itself. The large sea of sprawling buildings and dingy side streets teemed with people. Trishaws rang their bells loudly as they wove their way around us and through the moving crowd. Occasionally, the contents of a bucket, aimed at the storm drains below, would be thrown from windows overlooking the street. Even the bright coloured signs with Chinese or English lettering did not seem to remain still as they sung out from

18

above shops or along doorways. It seemed that this was a city which never caught its breath and could not be calm.

It was towards the end of the day, having had a fill of the city's desperate clamour, that we made our way back to Changi and the Malcolm Club. The Malcolm Club was sited at the edge of the camp and was solely for the use of camp personnel. We joined the group of airmen who had been on the beach the day before. They were sitting around a table in one corner of the large bar. Everyone relaxed, smoked and drank Tiger, a local lager-type beer.

There was a group of service women, or nurses, sitting nearby. Among them was a beautiful Eurasian girl. She had long hair which shone blue-black and hung in waves over her shoulders, rather than straight in Chinese style. She wore a brightly coloured embroidered Malayan blouse with a high collar around her throat. She looked across the room with dark almond eyes. Brian followed my gaze and thought he could read my mind.

'Lovely aren't they?' He leered in glee. Then with exaggerated concern, 'Pity about the sunburn, Chas.'

I glared back at him and said, 'Do they always go around worrying about everyone else in the valleys?'

The last words were mimicked with an exaggerated Welsh accent but he was in an exuberant mood. He was encouraged on by one of the others, who nodded towards a miserable looking man, a medical orderly who had been sitting at the table, quiet and withdrawn.

'Don't worry Chas,' said the airman, 'the part that matters isn't burnt. You could do better than him.' He looked towards the medical orderly and went on seriously, 'He caught his cock in his fly zip two days ago. Had two stitches in it. Didn't you mate? He has really got to control himself. It would be very dodgy if he got an erection before the stitches come out.'

The medical orderly reluctantly confirmed the story giving more detail.

Brian re-aimed his concern, 'Oh dear! That's bad! But, if you're a medical orderly, why don't you take out the catgut and re-stitch it with elastic? That should do the job for you, up and down, up and down, as many times as you like.'

He wagged a finger over his beer by way of illustration, watching its movement as he did so with an intense and amused concentration.

The medic got up, without smiling, amid the laughter and left quickly and furtively, without a word.

'Something we said?' I asked.

'No,' came the reply. 'He had to make a quick get-a-way. His girl friend has just come in and he can't trust himself with her.'

An attractive, lonely girl stood in the doorway. She was looking around, searching anxiously amongst the crowd.

'Tell her to come and join us,' suggested Brian, his attention now completely taken up by the slim, confused blond in the doorway.

In my present burnt predicament, I had taken some convincing but now felt sure that there were other people far worse off than me. That night I slept like a log. The tiredness and the Tiger beer had caught up with me at last.

A few days later we were introduced to a Royal Air Force Hastings four engine aircraft, or 'Hastybird' as it was affectionately known. Its dull, silvery bulk sat squat on the runway. It had the red, white and blue RAF roundel on its side and its four large propellers were set, high up in front, at the ready. About eighteen people boarded the plane to Christmas Island. This included Brian, who was to travel to Hawaii via the island. It was a very different set up from the civilian aeroplane and everyone was now in tropical uniform. It was a mixed crowd of Army, Navy and Air Force personnel. We understood that the island was an unusual command where all three services were stationed together.

There was one lady in our midst, a no nonsense, strong-minded Australian, in her early forties. She wore a green scouting uniform and was hitching a lift to the next port of call, Darwin in Northern Australia.

There was no waiting. All followed a well-seasoned Staff Sergeant across the tarmac of Changi airfield to the Hastings. Everyone was seated and strapped in. The huge Hercules engines started. Then the Hastybird showed that it was, in fact, like most of those on board, in no hurry. Perhaps it had seen too much action in the past. It seemed to have a mind of its own. The plane juddered and the engines stopped immediately; the tail wheel had jammed and the order was given to get off. The Hastybird had decided there would be a 24 hour delay.

The next morning, the plane was boarded once more but it remained still. The back door would not close. It stayed stubbornly on the runway giving another day's delay. This pleased Brian, who had been seeing more than a little of the girl he had met in the Malcolm Club. A take-off was attempted again on the following day but this time the Hastings decided to make magneto trouble the excuse to linger for yet another day and night. It was not until the fourth attempt that it actually became airborne. The passengers felt jubilant that the Hastybird had been tamed. Most of them had every confidence in the machine; after all, it had a good track record. They had, of course, made enquiries about this in between boardings and delays.

The plane, however, was still in playful mood. This became evident within fifteen minutes of the point of no return, the position midway between port of departure and the port of arrival. It was here that a trump card was played; one of its engines stopped dead. There was no intercom system on board and the Captain addressed his passengers by sending around a hand written note headed 'read and pass on'. Even before everyone had read the note, the plane had already jettisoned a large quantity of fuel and was heading back towards Singapore at a reduced height, following the procedure for such emergencies.

In spite of all this, the landing was safe and very smooth. The fire and ambulance appliances lining the sides of the runway in readiness were not needed and there was a pretty blond girl standing beyond the perimeter of the airfield waiting to greet Brian.

The green uniformed Australian lady was the first to leave the aircraft. Hurrying down the landing steps, she looked drawn and strained and a little older that she had first appeared. Nobody could blame her; she had not been brainwashed, as had the rest of us, about the excellent safety record of the Hastings. Some months previously, we had been told, one had made a successful landing in Aden with a full cargo and on only one engine - we still had three engines in working order. The Australian left without a backward glance but with a parting shot, that made no attempt to be genteel and sounded something like, 'Well, that's it! Next time I'm going with bloody Qantas!'

Holdall in hand, she walked hurriedly across the tarmac and through the exit gate at the perimeter of the airfield. She was no doubt hot footing it to Singapore International Airport. It was a disappointment. She had looked tough in an Australian, independent sort of way. She had seemed to be made of sterner stuff.

The Hastings and the rest of its passengers enjoyed yet another 24 hours in Singapore before it eventually took off both safely and efficiently. Brian sensed that this was to be a final farewell to Singapore and, sure enough, the plane made Darwin by late afternoon. As the aircraft came safely in to land it crossed some men's minds that, had they been superstitious or thought to placate the temperamental plane earlier, they might have considered off-loading the green uniformed Jonah a little sooner. But our Welsh companion remained overwhelmingly pro-Australian and continued to approve of green uniforms, wholeheartedly.

The airport at Darwin was empty looking. The wily Hastybird joined a few old Australian Air Force Canberra jets to one side of the main airport. Other than that, there were only some small light aircraft and one passenger plane in sight; it looked more like a semi-deserted airfield than an airport of any note.

At customs, the first thing that confronted passengers was a large notice hanging on the wall which read: NO FRUIT, SEEDS OR OBSCENE PUBLICATIONS AL-LOWED ENTRY. I felt guiltily conspicuous; my bag contained an orange and a copy of *Lady Chatterley's Lover*. The book had made recent legal history in the British high courts; the publishers had won their case to print the book in its original form, complete with explicit descriptions of sex and four letter words. I was halfway through the book and did not want to be deprived of it, so I walked slowly through the customs area with studied nonchalance - and was not stopped.

We had been looking forward to the night in Darwin. Hastybird willing, we were to leave early the next morning. So, after dropping bags in the Hotel Darwin, we set off to see the town. Darwin was a cowboy town come to life. Some aspects of it were like scenes from a Western movie. The wide roads had gaping, distorted cracks on the surface and the pubs had bat-wing doors. A further look at the area revealed that many of the houses, just outside the town, were supported by stilts at the front. The stilts were so high that cars were garaged underneath. The surrounding countryside stretched off in the distance as far as the eye could see. It was a vast, ambling, dusty and empty country.

The shops were closed at this time of day so we elected to go for a beer. Everyone had seen, in films, how to approach a bat-wing door. We knew exactly how it was done; you stroll up boldly, like John Wayne, peer over the top, look purposefully from side to side, push your way through the middle and walk slowly to the bar. We approached the doors with confidence but were immediately disappointed. The whole thing became a mess when five men tried to go through. The recoil of the doors, springing back into position, hit the person behind in the chest and we lost the effect. It was concluded that a cowboy's life had to be a lonely one, if only to get through bat-wing doors with some machismo left intact.

The man behind the bar had a face like a dried prune and a smile like a tight shoe.

'Wadda ya poms drinking?'

'Does it show?' Brian asked, looking surprised that anyone could even consider him a foreigner. The Australian looked along the line of faces until someone volunteered politely,

'Have you got anything resembling a beer?'

The barman looked back with deadpan expression and produced five glasses which were about the size of a third of a pint. He filled them slowly with a pale lager type of drink.

'How long you fellas here for?' He asked, managing to sound as though there might be some difficulty fitting another five people into his gigantic country.

'Till about six in the morning,' I replied, taking my first sip of the brew and detecting a glimmer of satisfaction on his poker face. The others tried their beer.

Brian stared into his glass, 'Could have done with staying in the barrel a bit longer,' the Welshman said.

'Like forever,' someone mumbled.

There was no one else in the bar and the atmosphere was frosty for such a hot place, so glasses were drained, bush hats put on and we ambled out.

Back in the hotel, Australia continued to hint at its size and abundance - which more than made up for the taste of its beer and the unenthusiasm of its welcome. The largest T-bone steaks that could be imagined were served at dinner. Each was so massive that it covered an entire plate, even overlapping the edge in places. While eating, we cut out a rough model of the Hastybird from a paper napkin and began to stick toothpicks in it, 'Another day here, *please.*'

The longer it took to get to Christmas Island, the better. The twelve months' tour of duty began the day of leaving the United Kingdom and more than a week had passed already.

But the Hastybird was beginning to develop a sense of purpose and, on the following day, it was not willing to pander either to our wishes or attempts at witchcraft. Its engines roared to life defiantly. It charged down the runway and leapt up into the bright, clear blue sky. But we were not too disappointed; there was to be another stop in Australia and after six hours the plane touched down at the Royal Australian Air Base at Amberly.

Here, shortly after landing, a bunch of unruly 'Aussie' airmen, came over to the Hastings and casually lounged around the landing steps, as though they had never been in a hurry in their lives.

'Hey ya pommy bastards, come and have a drink with us!'

They were friendly and relaxed. We got on very well with them. One of them suggested that we go back to his house to 'meet the missus.'

'It's only a couple of hundred miles down the road, mate.'

He had never seen anyone from 'the old country before' and neither had his missus. Our parochial minds pondered over the idea of 200 miles being down the road and we told him that we would come the next day if the

25

Hastybird played up. But it never did; it kept us away from the outback and took us straight to Fiji without so much as a hiccup.

It was only a night stop at Fiji but it was here, as though to mark the length of time since the sunburn and Singapore, that I began to shed skin. Whole sheets of it pulled off, intact, to reveal the new and vulnerable white covering underneath. When the Hastings took off, at five in the morning, there now seemed no hope at all of the plane misbehaving as it soared high above the steamy Fijian mountains. There was just one more lap of the journey to go and the Hastybird now seemed determined to get all on board to the destination. For the next seven or eight hours there was just sea below, and more sea. The massive Pacific Ocean.

As the hours passed, the Hastings became a sensible stalwart and surrounded all within its grey confines with a droning envelope of reassuring security. But, this did not go on completely uninterrupted. The plane had one last small game to play, with the help of air turbulence. Turbulence is caused when warm air rises and cold air descends rapidly, to take its place. It sometimes makes aircraft shudder and drop suddenly and the effect on passengers can be discomforting and unpleasant.

The toilet compartment on the Hastings was situated at the tail end of the plane. It was small but adequate. On this long flight, the only exercise that could be got, was the short walk from seat to toilet and back again. This gave some relief to stiff muscles and joints unused to being kept immobile for so long.

When the turbulence hit, I had spent about five minutes in this small cubicle and thus missed the hand written warning note that had been passed around. It was pure luck that upon leaving the compartment, my hand was gripped very firmly on the handle of the door.

The aircraft's drop came quite suddenly. I managed to maintain a hold on the door but my legs shot upwards. It

26

was like a fast descending lift. Every time it was possible to try to stand up, the same thing happened again and my legs shot from beneath me. This happened time and time again and I became resigned to the situation. I slowly lowered myself to the floor, hand over hand, while gripping the edge of the toilet door for dear life.

Four of the relief crew were about 8 feet away. They lay on inflatable air beds, viewing events with amused indifference. The turbulence did not bother them in the slightest. In fact they enjoyed it. They were repeatedly lifted, as if by some magical power, two or three feet into the air and then dropped down again onto their airbeds. It seemed to be a long, long time that I was trapped in that ridiculous position looking at the laughing relief crew and, beyond them, meeting the concerned, but fascinated gaze of the passengers, who all sat facing the tail end of the plane and watching the performance.

It probably lasted no longer than fifteen minutes but when I eventually arrived back at my seat, still feeling conspicuous, Brian asked, 'Taken to hanging onto the shit-house door for a bit of fun now have we?'

I wondered if anything ever went wrong for him.

The aircraft descended and banked steeply on its approach to Christmas Island. The island looked impressive from the air but at this height it could not be seen in its entirety. It was a large island. Green vegetation dripped into the deep blue sea on one side while, further along the coast the bare coral sand was showing its teeth.

The aircraft made a final approach and it was early evening when it landed on the island's only airfield. The reliable, but contrary, Hastybird rolled up to the shack-like terminal block. Doors were thrust open and steps put into place. Grabbing baggage, we took our leave of the plane. And that was how I finally set foot on this coral outpost, known as 'The Rock'; at precisely 7.30 pm on the twenty-seventh of November 1961.

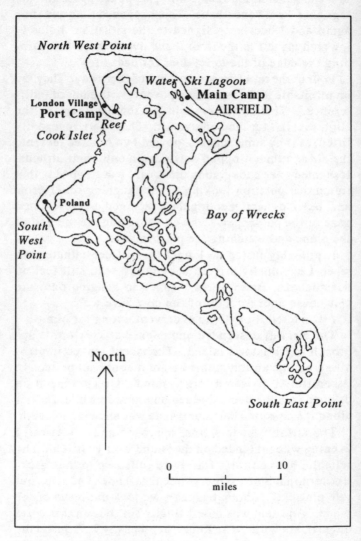

North West Point

Water Ski Lagoon
Main Camp
AIRFIELD

London Village
Port Camp
Reef

Cook Islet

Poland

South West Point

Bay of Wrecks

North

0   10
miles

South East Point

Christmas Island 1962

CHAPTER FOUR

The island

Christmas Island lies in the West Central Pacific Ocean, about ninety miles north of the Equator (1°52N, 157°20W) to be exact. It is the largest coral atoll in the world with a circumference of about one hundred miles.

According to Darwinian theory, coral atolls are structures remaining from coral-clad volcanos, long since disappeared with movement of the earth's crust. Hence they tend to be ring shaped land around central wells which have formed into lagoons. Coral reefs edge the atoll above and below the surface of the sea. Christmas Island looks as though it was, perhaps, formed around a range of volcanoes, rather than a single structure, because its ring of land is elongated at the south-east point; an area which is peppered with small lagoons.

The island is part of the Northern Line Island Group which lies within the British Crown colony of the Gilbert and Ellice Islands. The name it bears derived from Captain James Cook who discovered and charted the uninhabited island on Christmas Eve in 1777.

The island took on a tug-of-war history when, nearly eighty years later, the United States of America laid claim to the island, under the Guano Act of 1856. America wished to exploit the rich layers of bird droppings, or guano, which lay on the island. It was to be shipped to the United States for use as fertilizer. Great Britain did not recognize the American claim and proceeded to annex the island in 1888. British sovereignty was again challenged by the United States in 1936 and ownership has remained in dispute to this day.

There is an abundance of coconut palms on the island and a large, government-owned copra plantation employs a workforce of Gilbert and Ellice islanders who had been imported onto the island for this work. A British District Commissioner was in residence as well as the appointed Chief of the Gilbertese inhabitants.

The climate is tropical and the humidity extremely high. You are continually covered in sweat and materials go mouldy very quickly in such conditions. Any equipment rapidly deteriorates if not cared for properly. The heat and humidity would be unbearable were it not for the constant trade winds which continually fan the island.

From the first moment of my arrival, the island seemed ready to fulfil fantasies of Captain Cook's Pacific forays. On the drive from the airfield, the amber rays of the setting sun were being rapidly swallowed by the oncoming night. The palm trees became sharp black silhouettes against a wide orange and red sky and there was a sensuous beauty to the place. We peered out of the bus window while it trundled along the road and, as darkness finally closed in, we fell silent as though to register the self-aware loneliness of new arrivals.

The bus passed through the little village, nostalgically named London, where the Gilbert and Ellice Islanders live. It was dark now but, even so, the shadowy images of their dwellings could be made out. The dull glimmer of light from the village lit the palm thatched roofs. Some of the huts were built on short stilts while others had roofs which sloped low in front to form open porches. It was a haphazard cluster of different shapes and sizes which looked as though it had not been built but had instead sprouted from the ground along with the tall palms that grew around the village and between the huts. Our destination, Port Camp, was only half a mile from the village of London and it was not long before, with a grinding of brakes, the coach pulled up at the end of its journey.

In these exotic new surroundings, we felt prepared to meet the unexpected. We were not to be disappointed. As soon as the bus stopped, a strange rhythmic chanting was heard. Men peered out of the coach windows into the darkness. There were a number of half-naked, deeply bronzed figures alongside the bus: a hostile crowd, which started to wave arms and clenched fists, aggressively. Then they began to leap up and down, gradually working themselves into an animated frenzy.

They moved, rhythmically, to the beat of a deep throated, menacing chant, 'Moonies! Ahh moonies ! Ahh! I smell white flesh!'

In between chants, they sniffed loudly and rolled their eyes in affected hysteria. The bus passengers looked at them, bemused, for a few moments. If these were meant to be frenzied natives, they were not totally convincing, despite the energetic efforts. Fair hair and crew cuts, amongst the posturing heads betrayed their act. We quickly overcame our surprise and grabbed baggage to leave. We reached the door of the bus and Brian paused and looked loftily over the chanting heads.

'Take me to their leader!' he dramatized, his haughty tone bravely oblivious to danger. It was an obvious attempt to impersonate Captain Cook.

'They're all raving mad,' I said dryly, in much the same manner as the sea explorer's mate might have done. 'I wouldn't ask too much of their leader if I were you.'

We swung down from the coach door and were now in the midst of the excited bunch. A voice was calling my name. I answered loudly and an open hand was thrust out above the crowd.

'Rob Turner,' said the owner of the hand. He had the look of someone who had just won a major prize in a competition. 'Thought you weren't going to make it for a while, what with all the delays in Singapore. We always do this when replacements arrive,' he explained.

'I can go home now you're here; you're my moon, my replacement, my pale moonie. I really thought you'd never make it.' He paused and became the only still figure in the moving throng.

He viewed me with satisfaction and then stooped to pick up the baggage. 'Give us your bags. I'll take you to the room, not too bad, only four to a room. Come on, this way....'

He pushed a way through the small crowd. His chatter went on unceasingly; it was like meeting the character Ben Gunn from Treasure Island. Twelve months in this place and perhaps we could all end up as strange.

Rob led the way, about one hundred yards, to a rectangular building. An open porch covered the entire length of this long wooden hut. Six doors, opening onto the long verandah area, showed that the block was divided into six rooms. Rob pushed one of the doors open with his foot and, with a movement of his head, beckoned me to follow him through the door. Inside the room, there were six beds, although only four of these were in use. Beside each bed was a locker-type wardrobe and a desk-height chest of drawers. The walls were littered with a tantalizing collage of glamour girl pin-ups. Some of the pictures were new and glossy, others faded and old, their turned and tattered edges suggesting they were a legacy from bygone years.

Two men sat at a rickety wooden table, with large mugs of steaming tea in their hands. Coils of cigarette smoke hung lazily in the air. They cast envious glances at Rob and I nodded in their direction. The first to introduce himself was a slim man who was slouching low in his chair scratching lazily at the crotch of his shorts.

He interrupted his scratching and offered me his other hand, 'Brum,' he said concisely.

The other man stood up. He was broad shouldered and an unbuttoned shirt was tucked untidily into the waistband of his crumpled shorts. He had a fierce looking face and a strong bearing, which managed to hint at controlled defiance. When he talked, it was in the well-spoken tones of a Scots Highlander.

'I'm Jock to this lot around here,' he said, shaking hands. Then he nodded towards Rob, who was now engrossed scribbling and filling in the last square of a wall chart. It was a large home-made calendar placed above his bed. It was labelled 'Chuff Chart' in large, sprawling letters.

'I'm afraid you have to struggle to maintain a degree of normality around here,' the Scotsman explained seriously.

Rob finished working on the calendar. He cupped the back of his head with clasped hands and sank slowly back to view his work. He had a smile of supreme satisfaction on his face, like an accountant who had just balanced the books. It was clear who had been his missing number.

I looked away from the crowing Rob and back to the Highlander whose serious face surveyed me intently. Then suddenly, and surprisingly, it erupted into a gleeful, almost wicked, smile as he shrugged his shoulders and said, 'Welcome to the arse-end of civilization.'

Jock's label for the island made little sense at that time. His description seemed harsh. But then, he had been on the island for two months. This amount of time had already generated a claustrophobic impatience in him. He was intolerant of anything that came between him and freedom. He was always scathing in his dislike of the place.

But, at this first meeting, Jock gave the impression that I was a temporary relief from boredom. He willingly took it upon himself to introduce the surroundings and kept up a constant supply of information.

'The quality of the food varies with the amount of alcohol that the cooks take in from time to time,' he said as we went to eat. 'You will, perhaps, get used to the erratic nature of their talents.'

He handed over a tin tray, divided into three compartments, which he took from the top of his chest of drawers.

'That is what you eat from,' he said disdainfully.

'I thought they went out with the ark,' I said absent-mindedly turning the tray to study its edge.

'Oh, indeed they did,' he replied. 'Indeed they did. But unfortunately, the tide seems to have brought them back again doesn't it? There's no plate wash, that's the excuse. The officers' plates are hand-washed by the Gilbos but we wash these things ourselves. One thing though, just don't let our generous, catering staff overfill the compartments, or you will have one hell of an unappetising mess to eat.' He laughed as he spoke but beneath the good humour was an edge of well-educated resentment.

After the meal, Jock led the way to the single storey NAAFI recreation building. It was ideally situated, at the edge of a large lagoon. Blue and red topped wicker tables and chairs were scattered about both inside and outside, near to the water's edge. The clatter of beer cans and noisy chatter were in direct conflict with music being pounded out from an Hawaiian radio station. Cigarette smoke billowed out from an array of open louvre-type windows. The smell of beer wafted close behind it.

'They've only got Red Barrel in at the moment.' Jock said, as he lounged against the bar and ordered two drinks. 'It's canned and warm. Never had beer in a can before I came to this place - tastes better from a bottle.' He bought some cigarettes. They came in a large, round tin of fifty. He offered a cigarette then took one himself.

'Trouble with these things is they make you look as though you've got a permanent hard-on,' he grumbled as he crammed the tin, an unsightly bulge, into his pocket.

He passed over the drink, picked up his own pint and indicated the way through a partly open door, which led to the snooker room.

The room was a strange sight. The top of every surface was covered with a light coating of coral dust. The place had the appearance of an abandoned home that had been draped in dull white sheets and put into storage.

'The bloody dust and sand gets everywhere; the NAAFI Manager has the table cleaned once a week but, with all the louvre windows about, the wind just blows the stuff back again.' He moved forward and picked up an extension cue which was lying on the table. It had been cut in half and the other half was propped against a table leg.

He sharply cut off any objections. 'If you fancy a game, it's this or nothing,' he said. 'Don't worry, with practice you'll be able to miss most of the ripples on the baize.'

He slapped the table and sent up a puff of coral dust around his hand. I began to wonder, whether it would be possible for me to settle, along with the coral dust, into the same, indifferent acceptance of such, untidy imperfection.

Later that evening, in the billet, further doubts crowded in. Rob declared that he would be handing over his shifts to me the next day. He raised his hands above his head, then attempted to perform a cartwheel. The table, with Brum crouching close to a table leg, somehow got in the way. Rob's bent, ungainly legs came untidily in to land. He stubbed his toes noisily. Uttering a stream of oaths, he hobbled towards a bed. He spent some time shifting things around him but eventually, in an attempt to quell the excitement, he settled down and began to read. After a while, he put down the book, looked towards me and smiled contentedly. He patted his packed suitcase, hugged his kit-bag and finally went to sleep.

In the morning, nearly every trace of Rob had disappeared from the billet. All that remained to register his year-long stay was the discarded chuff chart. Scribbled squares completed, it gloated triumphantly down from its space on the wall.

I had one last sight of Rob, a short while later. He was already seated in the bus which was about to depart for the airfield. He had taken up position there a considerable time earlier. Brian was about to board the same bus, to continue the journey to Hawaii.

'No doubt we'll be in touch over the morse key very soon,' Brian said, as we approached the bus. The Welshman tried, perhaps for the first time, to sound a little apologetic for his good fortune. But, as we shook hands, it was easy to picture his arrival in Hawaii. He would be very much in place there, happily basking in his fate. He would enjoy it to the full, as dusky Polynesian girls surrounded him on all sides and, laughingly, competed to place more heavily-flowered leis about his garlanded neck.

I wished him good luck as he went. At that time, we were not to know that he would return to the island. We could not have guessed at the unforseen circumstances which would then surround us. I turned and walked back along the road towards the verandahed billets. In the daylight I could now see the area and the buildings, which were to become so familiar in the months that were to follow.

CHAPTER FIVE

Christmas on Christmas Island

It did not take long to get to know the Port Camp area where the island curves around like a giant claw, with the deep blue sea on one side and a beautiful pale turquoise lagoon on the other.

Looking out across the lagoon is St George's Church. The church is a substantial building, constructed by Royal Engineers, out of large blocks of coral, cut to shape and cemented together in a style not unlike the small stone churches in rural England. Much lighter in colour than the sombre grey of most English churches, the off-white building looks grandly serene in its tropical setting. The interior is immaculately kept. Plaques, hung on the pale coral walls, serve as memorials for servicemen who died during their term on the island.

Jock and I spent many hours at the church, not because of any religious fervour but because of an interest in music. The only good piano on the island was housed in a little room at the back of the church. Luckily the padre was an affable and good natured man. He did not seem to mind the noisy, secular music which often disturbed the tranquillity of St George's.

One evening, some weeks before Christmas, I was pounding out jazz for a number of listeners who were in this room, lounging about relaxed on easy chairs or reading out-of-date copies of *The Readers Digest*. A corporal technician leant against the piano and started to tap the lid to the beat of *Pinetops Boogie*.

My final chord of blues faded lazily from beneath vibrant fingers and he asked, 'How'd you like to present some programmes over at the radio station?'

He was one of a group of enthusiasts who were rebuilding the Christmas Island Broadcasting Service (CIBS); a small radio station which served the island. The project had been going on for some weeks and it was now nearly finished. He wanted someone to present jazz programmes. The Corporal was earnest and enthusiastic about the work. In any case he gave no chance to object to his ideas. Almost at once, he was leading the way, a few hundred yards, across to the radio station.

Entering the studio was like walking into the depths of a cave. The walls inside the building were almost completely covered with egg boxes.˙This lining soundproofed the studio and gave the interior a dull-grey colour and rock-like texture. As the door opened, a refreshing shock of cool air rushed out from the room. This was the only building in Port Camp to have air-conditioning. Here would be a chance to occupy the mind and gain a refuge from the heat. It would be a cool and comfortable retreat.

'It's new. It's only just been rebuilt,' explained the Corporal technician. 'The old station burned down. It's taken six weeks to rebuild. We've restocked with new records and programmes.'

He stopped talking. He was reluctant to give any more information about what had happened to the old station. This reluctance made me curious, as well as slightly suspicious. I pressed him to give more details of the fire.

'You know the fire station is just opposite here?' he finally explained, nodding in the direction of the fire-station. 'Well, when the old place caught fire, an emergency call was put through to them straight away, just across the road.' He paused for a moment and then continued, 'Would you believe it?' He stopped again to accentuate his indignation. 'The fire engine went round the Port Area three times, before anyone discovered where the fire was?'

There was a general disbelief in such inefficiency. There never were any reasons forthcoming as to why the fire appliance had made so many circumnavigations. Rumours abounded about the inability to find the fire. There was even some suggestion that it was a reflection on the type of programme being produced.

The rebuilding of CIBS was swift, defiant and carried out with some determination. The date of the new station's opening broadcast was to be Christmas Eve. The Corporal made it clear that, in exchange for the work and comfort of the studio, there was only one main obligation. The priority of all radio presenters would be to please the listener.

'That,' he concluded with positive logic, 'should keep the radio station standing.'

In those early weeks, it was hard to get used to this kind of undisciplined attitude and to accept certain conditions that prevailed in the camp. It had not taken many days on the island, before I noticed a dark brown speck in bread that had just been cut, ready to eat. On closer inspection, I discovered it was one half of a brown beetle.

I discarded the offending portion with some disgust. There was a plentiful supply of freshly-baked, crusty bread. It was piled on racks, in the mess bread room. So, using the bread room, cutting machine, I began to slice another loaf. Further examination revealed that each slice contained a number of unwelcome bodies, of varying species. I returned to our table with a pile of the bread.

'Look at this lot,' I said.

Jock held up a piece of bread and studied it from all angles, before declaring, 'There's a weirdie's arse and a leg in this one.' He picked up another slice. 'They can't all be like this.' Then he exclaimed, 'Good God! There's at least six legs and a head in this one too.'

He got up and walked over to the bread room. Ten minutes later, he returned with the news.

'I've just cut the lot up. They're all like it.'

He sat glaring at the bread.

'Good evening. Any complaints, chaps?'

It was part of the orderly officer's daily routine to walk around the airmen's mess and enquire whether there were any justifiable complaints. On this occasion, the beetles seemed worth mentioning.

'It's the bread, sir!'

The officer turned his head to one side and wore an expression of 'pray continue' on his face.

'All the loaves contain dead beetles, sir.'

There was an air of patient lethargy about him, as he replied, 'Oh, really?'

The officer led the way over to the bread room. He picked up a few of the mutilated slices and held them up to the light. He appeared to be talking to himself, as he remarked with fascination, 'So they do. So they do.'

Then he added in a positive vein, 'Most interesting. Had this before, you know; sometime back. Not much you can do about the little beggars - at least they're dead! May I suggest you, er, pick out the offending, little creatures, with your fingers, and, er, carry on like that, eh? Otherwise, it's jolly nice bread isn't it?'

His positive note had not seemed worth answering, so the complaint was left at that.

The weeks, leading to the Christmas opening of the radio station, passed by slowly. During this time, I did, in fact, begin to settle down, along with the coral dust. I gradually succumbed to the way of things on the island, although the lackadaisical manner of the RAF personnel was unlike anything encountered in the United Kingdom. There were only about 200 servicemen there at that time: approximately 120 airmen, 40 Royal Navy personnel and the rest were soldiers of the Royal Engineers. All were under the command of an RAF officer, who was known as the Base Commander instead of the usual title of station commander. It was understood that this was a throwback to World War 2, when Americans were stationed on the island.

The Army personnel though few, were, for the most part, of smart dress. Their weekly inspection parades were looked upon as a disciplined stand against deteriorating conditions about the camp. They appeared each week at one end of the football pitch; two sweltering rows of men in full tropical uniform, complete with heavy boots and knee-length socks. They stood under the hot tropical sun for about a quarter of an hour while their officer satisfied himself that they were not slipping into Pacific Island apathy.

The Royal Navy did not fall too far behind when it came to keeping up standards. Their rooms, immediately behind our billet, were cleaned out every morning. They wore colourful sarongs while doing their daily chores. This made for sly comments from our motley looking bunch.

'I really fancy that one in the blue skirt,' Brum ribbed wistfully.

Jock followed his gaze out of the window, 'You'll never get anywhere with her. Plays hard to get!'

'They can't all be bent,' I said to counter their prejudice.

'Put it this way,' Brum insisted, 'to walk around like that, he's got to be as bent as a fiddler's elbow.'

'What do they actually do here?'

'They unload the supply ships that arrive each month,' Brum replied, adding slyly, ' - among other things.'

'Oh - and the Army?'

'They are responsible for the laundry, the bakery and the like. And bullshit for the rest of the time, I suppose.'

It was true that there was not much work for any of us to do at that time, although we spent normal working hours in the communications centre. This was a grand name for the small wooden building situated on the edge of the lagoon, a few hundred yards from the church.

During working hours, the inviting waters of the lagoon could be seen through the hut windows but this did little to cool sweltering bodies in the heavy, overpowering heat which built up inside the hut's two offices. Constantly bathed in sweat, hands had to be continually wiped free from dripping moisture when using the morse keys, and message pads always became mottled with damp fingerprints. Because of its size, the communications centre was known as the WT shack, or radio cabin, by those who worked there. These numbered seven at that time; four airmen, two NCOs and a Flight Lieutenant. There was a shift system, although superiors worked days only, with no weekend duties. This left us working alone and unsupervised for some of the time, often in the cooler temperatures of the night.

It was here, in the radio shack, that I was working, in the overpowering heat of Christmas afternoon. Brian, on the morse key at Hickam, was exchanging seasonal greetings. He had heard the Christmas Eve opening, CIBS programme and was surprised that the small transmitter had reached a distance of over 1200 miles.

In the middle of the discussion, the Section Warrant Officer, unexpectedly, entered the radio cabin. We quickly cut off the message, because chatting in morse is against regulations. The Warrant Officer announced magnanimously that he had decided to take over the shift and told me to join the festivities taking place in the airmen's mess, where the Christmas tradition of officers serving lunch to the lower ranks was being nobly upheld.

The airmen's mess was a riot of noise and movement. To walk down the centre of the hall was to run the gauntlet of flying food and effervescent sprays of canned beer. Over to one side of the hall, Jock stood up and waved his arms to catch my attention. He motioned towards a spare seat at his table. An officer promptly set down a turkey dinner and placed some fresh cans on the table.

'Plenty of beer about,' said Jock. 'All by courtesy of Her Majesty's Government. The trouble is, the Army and Navy have had a fresh start on us.'

'Come off it, Jock,' slurred Brum, sitting opposite, 'You've been knocking them back quicker than they're being put on the table. Anyway, I thought you celebrated hog-mac-bloody-manay?'

Jock's eyes widened as he replied, 'Oh, I do. I do,' and with a satisfied look on his face, 'This is a bonus.'

The main noise level emanated from the centre of the hall. Here officers were efficiently serving cans of beer to soldiers, who immediately shook the cans up and sprayed the contents over their benefactors. They were making the most of their release from discipline. An Army Lieutenant, his beer-sodden shirt sagging about his shorts, was backing away towards our corner, quiet by comparison, as he tried to gain a brief respite from it all.

'I almost feel sorry for the poor sods,' commented Brum as he watched the Lieutenant's retreat.

Jock swore contemptuously at the statement. Brum glared back sullenly then pierced a can of light ale, placed his finger over the hole and shook the can vigorously. By crouching low on the floor and taking careful aim, he directed a jet of gushing beer up the inside leg of the retreating officer's shorts. The Lieutenant hit top 'C' on the musical scale, leapt into the air and swore.

Brum regained his seat and affirmed, 'As I said - I *almost* feel sorry for them.'

The incident was witnessed by some of the unruly soldiers who started to copy and conduct their own version of the vendetta. Brum, as the instigator, leaned back in his chair, looking very pleased with himself. Jock did not share Brum's satisfaction and mumbled his disgust.

'Don't tell me you disapprove?' I asked him.

'It's not that,' Jock scowled, 'I just hate to see good beer wasted.'

When the hullabaloo had died down and the beer and food had run out, men picked their way through the debris and walked unsteadily out of the open doors. There was not an officer in the mess hall who had escaped unscathed but they took it good naturedly, with no animosity or anger. At the radio cabin, the Warrant Officer sat waiting. He no longer looked like an altruistic benefactor; instead, he looked comfortably middle-aged, contented and pleased with a sanctuary from the furore.

That evening, many attended the service at St George's Church. Songs of praise and Christmas carols resounded throughout the port area. Everyone was in good voice, voices that had, no doubt, been well-oiled in the NAAFI bar beforehand and which would most certainly return to the bar for replenishment afterwards.

At the end of the day, three men lay in an alcoholic daze in the billet. Drink had not managed to strangle Jock's tongue. He was explaining that the Greek philosopher Hippocrates had said that life without celebration is like a long, long road without an inn.

'S'right,' replied Brum as he tried to concentrate his gaze on a cigarette held between his toes. 'You know Hippos - Hippy's s'right.' His head swayed as he watched the smoke waft up from the end of his foot, 'Reckon we've been down the pub all night or something like that.' He trailed off quickly then waited, as if for recognition of a profound statement. He got no reply, so he turned over, co-ordinated his foot skilfully and stubbed out the cigarette on an empty beer can. He fell back into instant sleep.

Jock shrugged his shoulders and abandoned philosophy for the night.

The only note to jarr the enjoyment and short respite from the long road of claustrophobic monotony, occurred on Boxing Day.

Brum, fully recovered from the previous day's drinking, brought news to the billet, 'They are considering testing bombs here again next November.'

'Who's they?' Jock asked looking up from his book.

'The bleedin' Yanks,' Brum replied, 'I heard it on Radio Australia.'

Some time was spent discussing the information. Old tales surrounding the atom tests were brought out to air. Everyone had heard several rumours. These included a story which purported that one of the three coral pillars holding up the island had been cracked by previous atomic explosions.

'Whole bleedin' lot will probably slip into the sea, next time,' Brum concluded. Then he declared with relieved self-interest, 'Well it won't affect us, whatever happens - we'll all be gone by November.'

Brum's information was quickly put to the back of everyone's mind. It seemed of no immediate consequence. It was well and truly forgotten by the time, nearly a week later, that the Hastings brought twenty new arrivals to the island.

It was New Year's Eve and a lanky whiter-than-white Irishman was brought to the billet. He stood awkwardly in the middle of the room and looked bemused and bewildered by the customary greeting he had just received. He was young. He was too young to be a conscript. He explained that he had been a boy entrant and had signed on for twelve years. He was proud of the fact that, six months previously, he had passed out 'Telegraphist 2'. The newcomer was nicknamed with the obvious 'Paddy' and we made fun of his youth and his obvious pride for a while.

'Pity you're used to all that modern, up-to-date equipment,' Jock told him, 'because the stuff we've got here is as old as the hills. If you're left-handed you're really in the shit. You know, you need your left hand to tune the left control knob, while you write with your right hand.'

'But I am left-handed. What can I do?' Paddy asked naively.

'Indeed there is only one thing you can do,' Jock advised.

'You will have to find another part of your anatomy with which to write. I tell you what we'll help you decide which one to choose, during this evening's celebrations at the NAAFI.'

'New Year's piss up? Oh, I've already had one.' Paddy said with studied nonchalance. 'Had one last night in Fiji, the other side of the date line.'

Jock stared at him for a moment and then mumbled something about two Hogmanays under his breath, making himself sound reluctantly impressed with the young man. By the time I left them to go to the CIBS studio for a session as duty announcer, that evening, Paddy was enthusiastically discussing plans for the New Year's celebrations, in spite of his feigned indifference.

At the studio, there were various requests waiting to be looked at. Previously, these had always been from listeners wanting their favourite records to be played on the air.

The first note that was opened read, ' PLAY ANYTHING, ANYTHING AT ALL. BUT FOR GOD'S SAKE DON'T PLAY "HOW'D YOU LIKE TO SPEND CHRISTMAS ON CHRISTMAS ISLAND" ANY FUCKING MORE.'

The note was passed to one of the programme presenters.

'That's a pity,' he said after he had finished reading, 'I rather like that one.' For a moment he gazed at the note with disappointment. Then, with a defiant look on his face, he said decisively, 'Sod 'em. I'll play it anyway.'

The corporal technician, who had been peering over his shoulder, quickly interrupted, 'No you bleeding won't,' he said, 'I'm taking it out of the library. That record's an effing fire hazard and that's that.'

We continued to joke about the note, for some while, but the good humour soon found a crack through which to slip away. At about 6.30 pm the news that two soldiers were missing was received. An upturned boat had been reported drifting beyond the reef.

I left the studio at 7.00 pm and stood on the shore of the lagoon. I looked across to where it met the vast hostile ocean. Two Auster light aircraft and three LCM vessels were combing the area. The aircraft circled over the water and above the reef until darkness closed in. The throbbing diesel engines of the boats kept up a continuous, uneven drone and they searched until dusk. The island's mood had changed. It had grown anxious and menacing. It was as though beneath its warm and sensuous face, there had always been a threatening Goliath ready to awake.

One of the soldiers was eventually recovered from an islet near the reef, known as Cook Island. The boat had capsized in the turbulent waters close to the treacherous reef and he had managed to swim the two hundred yards or so to safety. He was treated for shock. The body of his companion was never found.

A few days later, a memorial service was held and a plaque was placed inside the church. It was put alongside the others on the pale, coral wall. During the singing of the last hymn, I looked away from the line of khaki uniforms and gazed across to the row of bronze memorials on the side of the church; the lonely squares for each name. This seemed to be a strange place to die; in such a distant land which contained no enemy except an alien sea.

A firing party paid a final tribute with a volley of rifle shots. It was a sad and ominous start to the year. The rifle shots echoed across the lagoon and from its shores seabirds rose into the sky. The island was a sanctuary for millions of birds; at the sound of the shots they formed dark clouds of flapping wings above the palm trees. I watched them and deeply envied them their freedom to move far away, as they soared slowly and majestically above the reef and out over the great overwhelming ocean.

CHAPTER SIX

The young men and the sea

After the boating tragedy, the base commander sent round a circular emphasizing the dangers of the reef. This did little to dampen enthusiasm for the warm and dangerous blue water which surrounded the island. We were from a nation of seafarers and this vision was too tempting to resist.

Along with sailing and water skiing, fishing was enjoyed by many. It was strongly advised that fish measuring over twelve inches in length should not be eaten. The explanation given for this was that fish exceeding this size might be contaminated by previous atomic tests. I often wondered whether the Gilbertese were aware of this; seafood seemed to be part of their daily diet.

One day, a great deal of excitement was generated when some of the keener fishermen caught two sharks in the large lagoon and brought them back to Port Camp. The sharks were about eight feet long and they were displayed hanging from a block and tackle for all to see. They were an impressive sight, with their cruel jaws agape revealing rows of wicked looking teeth. The two men, who had landed the catch, stood proudly beside them and photographs were taken.

'How did you catch them?' Paddy enquired.

The taller of the two men set about explaining, 'We took a boat out to the middle of the lagoon for a spot of fishing when we caught sight of these two buggers. I just happened to have my harpoon gun on board and bingo!

Bit of luck, really.'

There did not seem to be a lot of skill involved, unless modesty would not allow it. So, it was not long before Paddy and I were walking along the edge of the lagoon towards the small yachting marina with shark fishing in mind. We approached an airman who was putting the finishing touches, with a paintbrush, to the wooden hull of a boat.

'Morning,' I began. 'Nice looking boat.'

He wiped the sweat from his brow with the back of his hand and, after a short pause replied disdainfully, 'Can tell you don't know much about boats.'

He was right; I knew nothing about them at all. The boat owner put his brush down and took a cigarette from its tin.

'This thing is as old as Noah's Ark,' he continued. 'The paint is about all that's holding it together. Still beggars can't be choosers.'

We kept on the subject of the boat and pointed out that, even so, the craft was good enough for fishing.

'Oh yeah, I mean - don't get me wrong - it's not that bad, as boats go. It's just, well, seen better days.'

We then broached the subject of the sharks that had been brought in that morning and asked him whether he had seen them.

'Yeah, quite big 'uns,' he confirmed.

'Fancy a go at catching one?'

'Ever caught one before?' he questioned.

'Er, no,' I said. Then added, with buoyant enthusiasm, 'There's always a first time.'

'You've done plenty of fishing though?' His question sought confirmation in such a way that it might prejudice the whole idea to sound too negative. I told him that I had not caught anything for quite a while.

'What's the biggest fish you ever caught?'

I glanced at Paddy whilst considering how best to answer. His face told me that he had nothing to offer in the way of fishing experience.

'A stickleback,' I replied boldly.

Instead of the ridicule that was expected, the boat owner dismissed the admission saying, 'Oh, not that I know much about fish anyway - got a harpoon gun?'

Paddy suggested that a gun could be got from the NAAFI shop.

'Then we'll go,' he announced. As an afterthought he said, 'By the way, the name's Paul. You can get me at the motor pool.'

The last part of this statement was magic to our ears. It meant that he would have access to transport. Up to now we had been confined to the Port Camp area. We had wanted to see more of the island, including the deserted Main Camp area. There is no hiding the feelings of someone who is pleased with his lot.

Paul was no exception when he was asked whether he ever borrowed vehicles, 'Sometimes,' he explained, 'I'm a mechanic and the wheelies do need testing from time to time.' Then, with an exaggerated furtive glance from side to side, he added, 'Like every day, weekends and all, know what I mean?'

'Yeah, I'm Chas and this is Paddy. We're in signals and we both happen to be off shift next Saturday for a spot of shark fishing. Is that all right?'

Paul scratched his head before replying, 'Okay. But don't forget the harpoons.'

The acquisition of a harpoon gun proved harder than expected. The NAAFI manager was very apologetic. He said that he had sold the last one that morning. He explained that suddenly everybody seemed to want the guns and that he did not expect another delivery for two months.

There was almost a week to work on the problem. One airman in our row of billets possessed a harpoon gun but he was not helpful. He knew that the supply had dried up and it would be hard to replace his gun if it got lost. We then tried the Aqua Club run by the Navy, but the answer was the same.

We were beginning to run out of hope, when further enquiries led us to a bright spark named Alan. Of Latin appearance, with jet black hair and small bronzed frame, he was one of life's natural ferrets.

'Tell you what,' he suggested, 'near the football pitch there are some old abandoned railings just lying on the ground. I'll get them sharpened and put a few barbs on them. They'll be ideal.' He paused and added, 'If I can come along.'

We readily agreed to this and reminded him that we would also need some thin rope to tie on the ends.

'Leave it to me,' he said, looking pleased with himself. 'Leave it to me.'

Everything was prepared in good time. We met Paul at the marina and found that he had brought another airman with him, making five in all. Paul examined the makeshift harpoons critically, 'We're not Moby-fucking-dicks, you know,' he said as he picked up the harpoons and felt their weight and balance.

He looked into faces which eagerly sought approval. He cast his eye along the edge, felt the point with his thumb and said, 'Gotta get pretty close in to use these. Sharks'll probably swim off when we try to close in.' After hesitating for a while, he announced, 'Let's give it a go.'

The harpoons, a few sandwiches and some cans of beer were placed inside the boat. Under Paul's directions, it was gently pushed into the water and we clambered aboard. The yacht was made to carry two or three people but five somehow managed to fit in.

With his hand on the tiller and strong, broad face under fair hair blowing in the breeze, Paul looked every inch a sailor; he would have been at home on a Viking long boat. He gave out instructions with confidence.

'Only move about one at a time and when I shout 'down' those of you up this end, known as the stern, crouch as low as you can, otherwise you'll get a crack on the head from the boom.'

The small boat was well down in the water but Paul seemed unconcerned, 'More hands to bale out with,' he commented as he lowered the keel.

The boat lurched forward as the strong wind pushed hard against the canvas mainsail.

'We'll head for the centre of the lagoon first and have a look around from there.'

The little craft gathered speed when the foresail was put into position. I was enjoying the ride, if nothing else.

All eyes scanned the surface of the water which rippled constantly from the continual trade winds. There were no sharks to be seen as we circled the area. Paul handed the tiller to Alan and stepped forward to slacken off the mainsail. He then made his way to the front of the boat and took down the foresail.

'I'm gonna put the spinnaker up,' he declared. 'It'll give us a bit more speed.'

Paul removed the untidy looking bundle from under my seat and replaced the foresail with the spinnaker. With a pull on the rope, the huge sail cracked like a rifle as the wind filled every crevice. It hovered above the front of the boat like a giant kite and almost caught me off balance as the bow lifted up from the water. Paul regained his position at the tiller after re-setting the mainsail.

'If we spot something,' he instructed, 'pull this rope and the spinnaker will come down.'

Despite the excess weight, the little boat skimmed across the surface of the lagoon with ease. Leather sandals kept slipping on the wet deck and salt spray ran down bare chests as we leant over the side to get a clear view. At its widest point the lagoon stretched for some two miles. We were about two thirds of the way across when Paddy spotted what appeared to be the dorsal fin of a shark.

'Thar she blows!' he called out, in the tradition of the old whalers.

Paul called sharply back, 'Put a sock in it; you'll frighten the bugger away.'

'There's two of 'em together,' Paddy observed more quietly.

Paul steered the boat towards the dark shapes moving slowly in the water, at the same time giving instructions to lower the spinnaker. Unaccustomed hands fumbled at the knots and Paul said impatiently, 'Hurry up, or at this speed, we'll run over the buggers.'

The big sail came down rather awkwardly and landed, a crumpled sodden heap, in the water. We managed to pull it into the boat and, after a fashion, fold it so that it did not drape over the sides. At last we had a clear view.

'It's a bloody manta ray,' Paul scoffed.

'Oh! So it is!' I confirmed, feeling somewhat disappointed. Then, with renewed enthusiasm, 'That'll do. Nobody has brought back one of those yet.'

Paul did not seem to like the idea, 'You're joking! That bugger is eighteen feet across. If it gets under the boat and tips us in, I don't fancy our chances against getting stung by that bleeding great tail.'

After a short debate, however, it was generally agreed that we should 'give it a go'. Paul slackened off the mainsail and the small craft bobbed gently towards the basking manta. The huge, silk-black hulk lay unsuspecting, like a piece of flotsam on the light emerald green water, as we approached it from the rear.

Harpoons at the ready, Paddy and I stood at the bow waiting for what we considered to be the right moment.

'Look at the length of that bloody tail,' Paddy remarked. 'I don't fancy a poke in the eye from that.'

We were within twenty feet and decided that was close enough. With an irresponsible thoughtlessness there was no hesitation about what we would do. We were now natives of this place, primitive hunting instincts had surfaced.

Hanging on to the rigging with one free hand and taking careful aim with the other, I threw the harpoon as hard as possible. It found its mark to one side of the centre of the manta's back. A split second later, Paddy's harpoon glanced off the creature's spine and fell into the water. The rope, having been made fast inside the boat, quickly payed out as the manta ray left the water and leapt into the air, revealing a whitish underside. A cascade of water droplets rained down from its huge body. A wicked looking tail appeared only a few feet from the bow of the boat. It landed with a mighty splash, covering us with spray and violently jerking the boat forward at the same time.

Paul shouted out, 'Rope should have been longer.'

He quickly lowered the sail as the manta began to take us in tow.

'I wonder how far it will take us before giving out,' Paddy remarked. 'Should get tired after a little while pulling us lot around.'

'How about shoving another harpoon out?' I suggested, picking up another sharpened stake.

'No, don't do that, we don't want to annoy him.'

Paul's friend who had remained quiet and rather placid, until now, became animated. 'Annoy him!' he screeched out nervously, 'I should hardly think he's too happy about pulling us bloody lot. If he twigs what's happening, he might turn on us.'

I lay down the harpoon and lit a cigarette, only to have it put out again by the manta leaping out of the water and splashing heavily down.

Paddy looked at me and observed philosophically, 'It's more like he's caught us.'

'Well, you've got to expect a bit of resistance,' I replied.

'I hope this bugger isn't going to dive,' Paddy said loudly as he indicated towards the bow. 'The weight of that thing is pulling this end down quite a bit.'

Suddenly the manta stopped. I heard Alan say, 'He's had enough.'

Paul's friend suddenly looked cheerful and suggested, 'We can tow him in now.'

The optimism was short lived. Gently, very gently, the craft moved forward again. The big manta had had its rest. He began a long steady swim, with us in tow, across the lagoon. It seemed a long while that the little yacht moved passively across the manta's rippling domain. Then another leap from the water, followed by an almighty splash, gave Paul reason to call out, 'Anybody got a knife on them?'

'What for?'

'To cut the bloody rope with.' Paul was sounding a little impatient.

'What and lose our harpoon?'

Paul pointed out that we could not continue in the same way all day. We had already been on tow for over half an hour.

'It can't last much longer,' I said, 'Let's just see what happens.'

There was a moment's pause, then Paul said quietly, 'I'll tell you what's happening, if you haven't noticed it, your bloody ray is taking us towards the reef.'

We stood up, hanging on to the rigging. There it was. The reef was two or three hundred yards ahead and was easily identifiable by its white foam crest. It was seething, like a monster's foaming mouth waiting to swallow and engulf us.

'Who's got a bloody knife then?' I called out.

There was not one knife amongst us. Momentarily discouraged, we leant back in silence. Out in the lagoon, some way behind us, was a Gilbertese fisherman in his outrigger. He seemed confident and at one with the sea. He waved to us but did not seem to realize the predicament we were facing. Perhaps he even thought that we were deliberately playing with the manta. He steered his small craft over to one side and then headed back towards the Port Area. Dejected and teased by the fish, we could not find it in ourselves to wave cheerfully back.

Looking ahead again Paddy called out, 'It's turning!'

With his large pectoral fins flapping like wings to propel him through the water, the great fish completed a half circle, then he began to take us back towards the centre of the lagoon.

'What you might call a round trip,' Paul's friend said with relieved tension, voicing the momentary relaxation that everybody felt.

Somewhere near the centre of the lagoon the manta shot up, crashed down and remained still. The boat began to drift towards it. As the rope slackened, I tried to undo the knot that had been tied onto the clevis.

'We're gonna bump into it in a minute,' a voice called out. My hands fumbled with the sodden rope and I tried desperately to unscramble the frayed ends. I looked towards the ray. Its fins were moving slowly up and down although it was stationary. The boat was within two feet of its wicked looking tail. Suddenly the manta heaved up its back and the harpoon came out. Flapping its fins, the big fish glided away through the rippling waters. It seemed utterly unperturbed by events.

Without a word we kept our eyes on the creature until it was almost out of sight. Alan broke the silence, 'Well that's that! The one that got away!'

Paul reached for a can of beer and said with a degree of finality, 'Thank Christ!'

The manta had pulled us around for the best part of an hour. The whole episode had given a better understanding than could any literature lesson of Ernest Hemingway's immortal classic *The Old Man And The Sea*.

Somewhat subdued we landed together with beer and sandwiches, on the shore opposite Port Camp. We found consolation in the beer and fascination in the shallow sand pools which lay scattered all along the beach. These contained hundreds of puffer fish which lay stranded half in and half out of the water. The puffer fish would swell up when they considered themselves under threat and cover the shore like gently rocking balloons. When they were prodded, they shrank alarmingly making a popping and hissing sound as they did so.

We picked our way carefully along the beach. Although wearing sandals with thick leather soles, there was still the hazard of cuts and grazes from pieces of hard coral or from stepping on sea-urchins which lay about in abundance. Someone at the camp had recently stepped on one of these spiked shells and had needed three days' hospital treatment before he recovered. Finally, we even found our shark; a sand shark which was about three feet long. It was lying, quite well camouflaged, in a shallow sand pool. He was impaled through his dangerous looking snout with one of the home-made harpoons. He was considered fair compensation for all of our efforts.

After about two hours on shore, it was decided that we make our way back to the Port Area. By now the tide had receded and had left the boat 30 ft from the water's edge. We pushed the boat along on the hard, moist coral sand and were almost knee-deep in water before the craft was afloat. As we jumped aboard, a long moray eel wriggled along the sea bed near to the spot where I had been standing.

It was late afternoon and we had been out for about five hours. With both sails set and the wind behind it, the little craft sped across the lagoon to the Port Camp marina.

That evening there was an eager and impatient queue for dinner. Eventually we were confronted by the main meal of the day, fish.

CHAPTER SEVEN

An invitation to London

The challenge of finding ways to break the monotony of confinement within the small Port Camp area stayed with us continually.

There was a swimming lagoon which lay adjacent to the large lagoon by the church and swimming was popular. Sharks were kept out of the swimming area by a sand bar stretching across to separate the two lagoons. Here would be a perfect place to swim were it not for the fact that, sited on the sand bar, was the small-bore rifle range. Before taking a dip, it was necessary to make sure that the red flag, indicating target practice, was not flying. These less-than-brilliant logistics encouraged most people to take to swimming at the Spit (the name given to water near to where supplies were off-loaded).

To while away spare time in the evening men read and went to the open-air cinema as much as possible, although the cinema boasted a change of programme only three times a week and a number of stitched patches on the screen bore witness to the quality of some of the films that were shown. Inside the cinema, a notice on permanent display read: PLEASE DO NOT THROW BEER CANS AT THE SCREEN.

We escaped, at last, from the confines of the Port Camp area when Paul took a Land Rover from the motor pool for a tour of the island. We wanted to see Main Camp, the centre which had been used during the atomic tests, and this was the area we made for first of all.

The approach to Main Camp was along a dusty tarmac road. We neared the entrance of the camp and Paul slowed down. Main Camp covered a large area. It was reminiscent of a ghost town. There were a large number of buildings which must have bustled with life during the time of the 1950s tests. These now lay deserted. A pair of rusty iron gates at the entrance were partly open and hung limply from broken hinges.

After a brief glimpse at the abandoned camp Paul turned the vehicle into an adjacent side road. Here lay a huge scrap yard. It was in a large clearing, nestling among the palm trees. There were massive cranes, bulldozers, Standard Ensign saloon cars and rows of Land Rovers stacked two high.

'Worth a fortune that lot,' Paul said. 'Apparently it would cost too much money to send them all back to the UK. What a waste!'

Fascinated, we glanced over our shoulders at the rusting relics until they were out of sight.

A few hundred yards further down the bumpy road, we came to a large inland lagoon. A well weathered notice board at the water's edge announced: 'MID PACIFIC WATER SKI CLUB'. The sign was attached to a small boat house which housed skiing equipment and a motor boat. The place was deserted and inviting, so the morning was spent learning to water ski.

When everyone in the group could keep upright on the skis long enough to circle the lagoon at least once, we rested aching limbs and slated salty thirst with a lunch of canned beer. Then, after a while, we travelled on around the coast to a place which for some reason had been given the name Poland.

On the way to Poland we passed through the shade of the immense copra plantation. Friendly Gilbertese waved from the plantation. They could shin up the tall palms with great strength and agility; their muscular backs leaning against loops of rope which were attached around the tree trunk and which they moved upwards with them as they climbed. Large machete knives were used to cut open the tough green husks after the coconuts had been harvested.

On the journey back to Port Camp, we passed numerous inland lagoons. These included small pools coloured by marine plants. They were deep red and lay either side of the road like ponds of blood. There were also beaches of hard packed coral where giant crabs congregated. These whitish pink creatures were about the size of dinner plates and had pincers as large as a man's hand. They blended well with the colour of the coral. We got out of the Land Rover and walked down the beach to take a closer look at them. They were unafraid of our appearance and approached us with huge claws snapping noisily at the air; their sideways gait adding to their cumbersome, but impressive, appearance.

Paul stopped to concentrate on opening a fresh can of cigarettes but suddenly yelled, 'Ow! Bastard!' when one of the crabs nipped at his ankle.

Paul immediately raised one foot to kick at the offending pink shell but instantly changed his mind; he was wearing only flip-flops like the rest of us. We realized our vulnerability as more crabs, almost like reinforcements, started to converge on us in greater numbers.

It became a wild game of hop-scotch as we dodged our way back to the Land Rover. There were one or two yells as the crabs scored. One man slipped on a patch of wet sand. We piled into the vehicle and gazed down at the mass of crabs.

'Never seen so many before,' Paul remarked, 'Must be the mating season or something.'

'Well one of them certainly tried to fuck me,' answered the man who had fallen over.

'Good job he let go,' Paul said. 'It would be embarrassing to report sick with a dose of the crabs!'

That day we had travelled a distance of about 48 miles to Poland and back. When we returned to Port Camp, we felt satisfied that we had seen a good part of the island. But there was one restricted area of the island that we could not visit on that day or any other. It was prohibited to stray off the main road at the point where it ran through the tiny village of London.

The Gilbertese men left the village to work elsewhere on the island. Some worked at the camp performing mainly menial duties; they spoke very little English and we managed to communicate at only a very basic level. The Gilbertese women never left the village; at least at no time did we see them outside that area. No contact, of any sort, was allowed with them.

Paddy was the first to mention any yearning in the direction of this forbidden enclave. He confronted us one day full of concern; his posture slumped with discontent, 'There must be something wrong with me,' he glowered. 'I was walking past the village and I saw this Gilbo hanging out her washing. I really fancied her stretching up there putting things on the line.'

Jock raised his eyebrows, 'Best not to get any ideas,' he replied. 'Not only would their fellas cut off your balls with their big coconut knives, but the rest of you would be in for a court martial.'

Paddy regained his youthful exuberance. He winced and began to shuffle around the room, knock-kneed, with exaggerated and overacted discomfort.

This tempted Jock to add the comment, 'Mind you, they'd have to shin up those lanky legs first and they're not used to such wee coconuts. Anyway, if you want a closer look at the native females, there's a dance coming up at the village soon.'

This information was met with disbelief, until Jock explained that it was a tribal, ceremonial dance. This would be the only opportunity to get a closer glimpse of the village other than by invitation of the District Commissioner.

The evening of the dance eventually came round. We approached the village of London and a sound that resembled the beating of jungle drums added to the atmosphere created by the warm, still evening and large full moon.

The village was a ramshackle affair. Its huts were timber-framed with the broad leaves of the palm tree covering roofs and walls. Some huts stood on stilts a few feet off the ground to assist ventilation. A small Gilbertese cemetery bordered one side of the main road, with a low, white picket fence serving as its boundary. As we passed by it I wondered how deep the graves were because there could be no earth there, only coral sand, dust and rock.

The repetitive thumping grew louder. We stepped off the road and into the village, palm shadowed in the moonlight.

The magic of the moment was shattered by Paddy, 'I'm after thinking bloody Tarzan is going to swing through the trees any minute,' he said and he yelled a weak imitation of the jungle hero's call.

'You sound like a cat that's just been neutered,' Jock muttered. 'Anyway you might need Tarzan's help.'

'Why's that?'

'You know that old Gilbo that works in the bakery, the fella with the two teeth? Well, he told me that he actually ate human flesh years ago. He likes thumbs. They were cannibals until well into this century.'

'Didn't do his teeth much good,' Paddy observed. 'Tell you what if there's a suspicious looking cooking pot around we'll stand back to back and hold them off for as long as we can.'

Undeterred we proceeded and found our way to the large open-sided hut where the celebrations were taking place.

A large number of servicemen were gathered around the perimeter of the hut. The powerful drumming emanated from one corner, where eight Gilbertese men were squatted around a long oblong wooden box and were beating it with great gusto.

Paddy seemed determined to resist cultural influence. 'Looks like eight Gene Krupas playing on a coffin,' he said quietly.

The dancers were men, women and some of the older children. They were a colourful spectacle. They wore flowers and grass skirts. The atmosphere was that of an oversized family gathering and there was a creche of babies and very young children to one edge of the hut. This was supervised by a massive Gilbertese woman who fussed gigantically and warmly over the small brown children. Other women, skins shining with coconut oil sat amongst them threading flowers to make garlands. Most of the babies were sleeping but some moved quietly and happily on the brightly coloured blanket which formed a carpet in that corner of the hut. The small children seemed unperturbed by all the noise.

While we waited for the dance to begin, Jock pulled a can of cigarettes from his pocket. He offered them round and began to light his own. A Gilbertese man drinking from a battered enamel mug was standing nearby. He watched Jock intently then leant across and said cheerfully, 'E tabu te moko.'

Jock nodded back, smiled and put the cigarette back into its can.

'What did that mean?' asked Paddy.

'Roughly translated,' Jock replied, 'it probably meant, put that thing out, or else my grass skirt may catch fire. The grass hut may well go up with it too and don't forget the toddy I'm drinking can blow your ears off so that would help the flames on a bit as well wouldn't it?'

Some of the children now began to perform a melodious Pacific version of *It's a Long Way To Tipparary*. The strange mixture of the familiar and unfamiliar lulled me into relaxation. Then the women began to dance.

As they moved, the vividly patterned strands of material which hung from belts around their waists swayed more slowly and heavily than the lighter swishing grass skirt beneath. They wore circlets of white grasses on their heads which made their hair seem starkly black by contrast. Their throats were garlanded with leis of deeply coloured orchids and their arms, from shoulder to wrist were adorned with flowers. Thick petalled bands around their wrists and ankles made their hands and feet look small and delicate although, in fact, they were broad and strong.

As their arms swayed and turned in gestures of inviting openness, the gaze of their dark eyes followed the movement of the expressive hands. Some of the younger women had a shy, fixed gaze, as though they were concentrating deeply on the words of the song or the movements of the dance. They themselves looked like gently swaying flowers. The dance seemed to have always belonged here, like the trade winds and the ocean, the palm trees and the coral reefs.

Paddy gazed languidly at the seductive spectacle. He remained silent until the women had finished their first dance. Then, in a sudden conversion from his protestant roots, he scowled, 'Bloody missionaries, I bet they told them to wear the T-shirts.'

The Gilbertese men then joined in the dancing, wearing plainer headdresses and grass skirts. They moved fast and energetically to a more insistent rhythm.

When the display of Gilbertese prowess came to an end, there was rousing applause. We drifted back to camp reluctantly and Paddy seemed only slightly placated by the limited contact with women he had been allowed that evening.

Alone in the claustrophobic heat of the radio cabin, I stared at the morse-key and at black tuning dials set in dull grey metal. Thoughts came of lying down amongst heavily scented flowers and of dark brown skins and earth-coloured eyes. I had almost forgotten the touch of pale, elegant hands; I found it hard to imagine long brown hair which became gold threaded in a gentle sun.

I pulled myself away from melancholy and automatically switched on the kettle. I opened the night rations collected earlier from the cookhouse. A revolting sandwich of dried up bread appeared. Sweaty, molten corned beef lay between stiff slices of brittle bread. It was an impossible combination.

Something had to be done about the situation. An old, electric hotplate lay abandoned at the back of one of the cupboards. I pulled it out, examined it and found that the element was broken. It did not take long to repair and then clean. I set it on a table outside the radio shack where water and a kettle were also kept. The hotplate was plugged in and it worked. Tomorrow it might be possible to get a frying pan and see whether raw rations could be drawn from the cookhouse. The corned beef sandwich was abandoned and thrown outside the cabin. It would make a good breakfast for the grapple birds.

CHAPTER EIGHT

Brigadoon

The two months leading up to February passed slowly by. Untidy autonomy increasingly became the accustomed way of life as men relaxed in the equatorial heat. It was easy to drift far away from European striving and sink deeply into comfortable apathy; as though mesmerized by the roll of ocean breakers and the buffeting of continual trade winds. As much advantage as possible was gleaned from the degree of prevalent self rule. A short while after the electric hob had been repaired, permission was given to draw raw rations from the cookhouse. Immediately, with gourmet precision, a small store of food was built up in the radio cabin. It was more than adequate to develop an indulgent self-catering system. This was useful for night duties or any other time the melee of mass catering needed to be avoided.

It was into this easy-going atmosphere that a new Base Commanding Officer appeared. We knew of his arrival but the habit of reading Station Routine Orders had never become completely ingrained in the small group which shared the billet. We were unaware that the Commander was to be shown around the camp by the Station Warrant Officer and that his tour would start with an inspection of airmen's accommodation.

A working shift had finished late the previous evening and I lay in bed, naked, with right knee protruding through a long tear in the sheet. Jock sat drinking a mug of tea. Paddy was enshrouded in the usual cloud of smoke from his cigarette as he lay in bed with his shoulders propped up against the wall. He was reading a copy of the previous month's *Tit-Bits'* magazine. The billet floor was covered with a light film of coral dust. A number of buckled beer cans, together with old newspapers and various items of clothing, lay scattered about. At 10.00 am precisely, the door opened and the Station Warrant Officer, accompanied by the new Base Commander stepped into the room. Every man in the room froze.

The Warrant Officer stood stock still and surveyed the scene. He was a big, strongly built man who held regular weight training sessions on a section of the lagoon edge which had become known as Muscle Beach.

'Didn't you lads know there was an inspection this morning?'

His voice sounded strained. It seemed unlikely that the strain was anything to do with damage from body-building sessions. The mind raced.

Jock had been on shift during the night but he was the only one who now looked as fresh as a daisy. Luckily he was rested and quick-witted enough to say confidently, 'Er, we're all off night shift, sir.'

In the moment's silence that followed, no one was tempted to add more. Would the Base Commander know, or would he not know, that there was a one-man roster at night? It was impossible that all had been on shift.

The Warrant Officer picked up the verbal cue, at the same time giving no indication as to what else he was thinking. He turned to the Base Commander with a sigh, 'These lads work ever so hard, sir. Communications you know, 24 hours a day stuff.'

The Commander remained silent.

The Warrant Officer turned towards us again, 'Look, when you get the chance, not now but sometime today, give the place a bit of a dust out will you?'

With that he quickly turned and politely ushered out the Base Commander, whose face had just begun to show an expression of puzzlement.

Everyone in the room had remained stock still throughout the incident and now all eyes were focused on the door as it was closed behind the two men. A wave of intense relief echoed the closing of the door. The silence was broken by Jock as he slumped back in his chair, whistled loudly through his teeth, and let the mug of tea slip through his hand carelessly so that it splashed onto the table. The rest were still looking at the door in disbelief. When thoughts were finally gathered sufficiently enough to put them into words, we resolved to act on the Warrant Officer's suggestion. We would begin to clear up later on that day.

So began a new regime of order and cleanliness. Shortly after, as though to complete this new way of things, Captain Flit paid a visit. This was the name given to the pilot of the crop spraying aeroplane, which regularly sprayed the Port Area to keep flies and other insects under control. On hearing his approach, droning like a giant bee in the distance, everyone scrambled about closing doors and louvre windows. Men who were outside, in the open, immediately took cover in the nearest available room. The little Auster swept low overhead, spraying DDT. The pilot hedge-hopped over the rows of billets leaving a white trail of insecticide behind him. His skilful flying took him below the telegraph wires before he gained height and departed from the area. The spray clung to the windows like rain but, after a while, it evaporated in the hot sun.

'We'll all drop dead like bloody flies ourselves, one of these days,' Brum remarked.

'I can fly a plane,' Jock said as he looked vacantly out of the window and watched the Auster fade into the distance.

He sensed the unspoken questioning of his statement and moved towards the drawer of his locker. He got out a document and tossed it in my direction. It was indeed his pilot's licence.

'I need to get a number of flying hours in before twelve months are up otherwise I'll have to take another test, when I get back. That would cost too much.'

He gazed out of the window, as though searching for the plane that had now disappeared.

'I'd like to log up a few hours on the Auster. I've already asked once but they don't want to know. I might try asking again in a few months time.' He placed the licence back in the drawer. 'Wanted to fly when I came into the RAF, was one GCE short even to be considered.'

He started to mimic the voice of an arrogant, interviewing officer, 'How many GCE's have you got?'

'Four sir,' came the mock reply to himself.

'Well you haven't got enough then, have you? Next candidate.'

Returning to his own voice he said, 'And that was that. I must have been pissed when I signed on for the extra years.'

He sat down on his bed, lit a cigarette, picked up a slide rule from his locker, and began making imaginary air routes. The brief display of resentment was instantly absorbed by what he was doing.

After the new Commander's inspection, the billet's standards of orderliness began to show some improvement but, at the same time, those of the Royal Navy neighbours were gradually deteriorating. The first signs of this were noticed when a group, in morning-sarongs, were attempting to sweep their verandah; they were visibly swaying on their brooms, almost as though they were on board ship.

They seemed to have become sadly land-locked; the occasional forays out to sea only took place when large cargo ships dropped anchor beyond the reef. It was not often that the navy detachment was required to ferry supplies from the cargo ships, using their 45 ft LCM boats which could cross the reef with ease. It was noted with interest that the amount of time when the majority of them appeared sober was decreasing almost imperceptibly.

Their officer carried out his usual inspections. An air of normality prevailed at first whenever he was around: a tall, superior and intimidating man who usually appeared, immaculately dressed, in white, tropical uniform. He was nicknamed Captain Scuttle; a name which harked back to a time when, it was rumoured, he had an encounter which resulted in damage to one of Her Majesty's submarines.

We began to look forward to any developments and followed the progress of Captain Scuttle's visits with some fascination. On one occasion, just before his late-morning inspection, the door of the Navy billet burst open and an air of hilarity reigned inside. A slumping sound was followed by muffled laughs, someone peered through the door and signalled to others that the coast was clear. Then a limp body was pulled from the room. The group, dragging out the body, giggled and tripped over each other but even so managed to lift the load onto the concrete path and roll it neatly into a space near the verandah. They quickly shielded it from view with brooms, buckets and anything immediately to hand. The prone figure was hidden just before Captain Scuttle strode slowly and imperiously towards the billets.

'Look at that!' muttered Brum. 'What shall we do with the drunken sailor? And it's morning too.'

These events soon had everybody looking for explanations. Reasons did not seem to lie in normal beer-drinking sessions in the NAAFI neither did the traditional daily Navy tot of rum seem to explain anything. The free rum ration was allowed to accumulate and was issued every

Friday, when members of the RAF or Army were occasionally invited over for a drink.

Previously the Friday drinking had always been within reasonable limits but now, when Jock joined them one evening, he returned from the visit intrigued, 'I didn't stay long. They were all blown out of their minds. You can't enjoy a drink with anyone that pissed! They must be spending a fortune on the stuff; they had bottles of it stored everywhere, under the mattresses, hidden all over the place.' He stopped to contemplate the idea, then added, 'Funny thing, though, a lot of it didn't have labels on. Good stuff though. They're not manufacturing it, that's for sure!'

The noise and hilarity increased at a faster rate and Captain Scuttle's appearances began to occur more frequently. He poked around with questioning authority, searching doggedly for answers. It all came to an abrupt end on a riotous night, which was not at a scheduled inspection time. Captain Scuttle unexpectedly opened the door of the Navy billet and viewed the chaotic anarchy which reigned inside. The hut was full of men, too far gone into drunken stupor to worry about the sight of their commander, standing tall and immaculately white, in the open doorway. He stood surveying a scattered scene in which empty and half-empty spirit bottles, unlabelled and strewn around the room, sub-titled the boisterous decadence in front of him.

The developments were now wholly noticeable by their absence. The Navy billets fell into a contrasting silence. A little while passed before the full story emerged. It was finally learnt that certain members of the Navy aquadiving club had been at the centre of a conspiracy.

We had always taken it for granted that the divers were interested in the beauty of the teaming ocean life which lay in abundance about the island. We had assumed that search for marine knowledge and the love of sport had been their overriding motivation. This may have been true for some. For others, the thrill lay in swimming more devious undercurrents.

'It's a rum do all right,' Jock enthused with glee, when he first found out the truth. 'Or more like a case of whisky galore. The divers have been retrieving cases of spirits that have somehow just managed to find their way overboard the LCMs, near to the jetty. That's why half of them were permanently pissed. The labels must have come off in the water. I knew it was good stuff. The main culprit has already been court-martialled. He's been found guilty and is being sent off the island.'

'Lucky sod,' interjected Brum.

'Probably six months military prison in Singapore,' said Jock, sounding envious.

Everyone was left to wonder whether there was any justice left in the world.

Discipline returned to the Navy detachment and the diving club was channelled back towards legal waters. It was again presumed that the divers went back to an interest in marine life or to the love of sport. At the same time some of the noise and exuberance faded from certain nearby quarters.

On 4 February another darkness fell on the island. If we had lived in more primitive times, it might have been thought that what happened on this day was a foreboding of evil or a warning of impending disaster. But this was not the case; nobody had gone native to that extent and it was with more enlightened and scientific minds that they observed the total eclipse of the sun which took place.

A dark shudder was felt as the moon began to move slowly across the path of the sun's light. The blinding glare was sapped from the coral sand. The sparkle faded from the lagoon and the island gave a cool shiver as it was draped in an eerie greyness. Men peered through black photographic negatives to protect their eyes. What was happening was eagerly noted; times and observations were discussed with logical interest.

If deep rooted emotion had been allowed to invade minds for even a moment, perhaps they would have been engulfed by the overpowering feeling of timelessness of a place without the sun. Logical thought may have been consumed by fear of the supernatural. There would have been mystic connection made between the dusky space where they stood and the moon, sun and the universe. They may have felt the kind of superstitious terror and violent panic which could only be expressed by human sacrifice. As it was, they passed around the smoky black negatives to each other and noted that the eclipse lasted from 2.15 until 3.15 pm. They were modern men and did not believe in human sacrifice.

It was a strange coincidence that even to modern men ill-tidings did follow within a week of the eclipse. These came in the form of confirmation of news that had circulated back in December. The warning was brought by courtesy of Radio Australia.

Radio Australia broadcast world news and brought news from home, unlike the Hawaiian radio stations which seemed solely interested in news from the USA. It was enjoyable listening to the Australian announcers who were an amusing contrast for people brought up on a diet of BBC formality.

The announcer began that morning in his broad Australian accent along these lines, 'Good-day. This is Radio Australia on the air once again. It's the 7th February 1962. The main news this evening is that...'

He paused and cleared his throat noisily.

Then he went on in a matter-of-fact monotone, '......Christmas Island in the mid Pacific will once again see nuclear bomb testing. The United States will conduct a series of tests this coming November...'

The broadcast seemed to answer the question that had lain dormant, why there should still be a military presence on the island? This had only been for nuclear testing in the past; the island seemed to serve no other strategic purpose at all. At this stage it was thought the tests would have nothing to do with Britain. I was due to leave the island by 13 November at the latest. There was talk of an atmospheric test ban and although the news was registered no-one thought it was of much significance to them.

'They know more than we do sometimes,' Paddy observed.

'It's probably true enough,' said Jock. 'Let's face it, that's what the island's been used for in the past.'

'Pity the Yanks aren't arriving a bit earlier, then we could all bugger off home,' said Paddy. He also took it for granted that there would be no involvement in an exercise carried out by a foreign power. 'Anyway how come the Americans are coming to test their bloody bombs here. I thought this was a British island?'

The dispute over ownership of the island was discussed for a while, and Paddy was given some instruction on the history of the island. At the end of the lecture he observed with his usual youthful logic, 'Guano Act or no Guano Act, the Americans must be really mad if they want radioactive bird shit. Not the best of fertilizers I would have thought!'

It was during February that it rained almost non-stop for some days. It was not a familiar kind of rain; you did not need to hide under umbrellas or shelter from its cold penetration. It was torrential but had a welcome coolness. Its coming was celebrated by rushing outside clutching bars of soap.

'Bloody marvellous!' Brum spluttered through the water which ran down his face and dripped from his nose. The rain beat hard against upturned faces and shoulders and ran heavily down naked, gleaming bodies. The soft wet coral stung ankles as the open-air shower pitted the ground around moving feet. After much noisy yelling and splashing about in the rain the men from the billet stepped back into the room and towelled themselves dry.

'Couldn't do this at home,' remarked Brum.'Freeze your bloody bollocks off. Not to mention the neighbours looking on.'

'Mind you,' observed Paddy seriously, 'if you were a member of a naturist club you'd soon get hardened to it all.'

An evil smile spread across Brum's face, 'I'd get hardened all right, looking at all those nude girls.'

'You're just a dirty sod, Brum. I suppose when you get back they'll have to lock up the whole female population of Birmingham.'

'Too right they will. That's the price they'll have to pay for putting me here.'

'Lucky Birmingham,' said Paddy sarcastically.

The torrential rain continued, pouring wet sheets across the thirsty island.

It was still raining that evening as eleven customers sat on wet, dripping wicker chairs in the cinema, patiently waiting for the arrival of one more person. With an audience of less than twelve, there would be no show. Oilskins were worn and cigarettes smoked in wet, cupped hands. A cheer went up as the twelfth man arrived and the film could now begin. Immediately it started, the projectionist, housed in a tiny room at the rear of the cinema, turned up the sound to compensate for the noise of large blobs of rain which splattered off twelve black oilskin hats.

It had stopped raining that night when I set out at 11 pm, in the damp heat, to relieve Jock from his evening shift. Anticipating the usual quiet night's work, I carried a mug in one hand and a book in the other and had a pillow tucked under my arm. As I approached the radio cabin, the shrill staccato sounds of morse code reverberated through the still night air around the building. My first thought was that Jock might be using the practice key, in a frenzied attempt to alleviate his boredom but each step nearer suggested that he was receiving a live, coded transmission.

I flicked on the switch of the electric kettle and passed through the open door. Jock was leaning over the desk and had just acknowledged receipt of a message. He sat back and rubbed the palms of his moist hands along the sides of his trousers. Dark patches of sweat were visible on the back of his unbuttoned khaki shirt.

'Been busy as hell tonight,' he volunteered. 'That's the sixth long bugger that I've taken down in the last couple of hours, not to mention the four I've sent.'

I glanced at the secret coded message, 'This is a bit unusual isn't it? Since I've been here I haven't had that many signals in a week, leave alone a couple of hours.'

Jock indicated the pillow, 'Wouldn't mind betting that you don't get much sleep tonight. Sir is in his office unscrambling them at the moment.' Then he added, 'By the way, the uncoded good news is that a plate-wash has been dispatched from the UK. It should arrive by late July. It's probably coming all the way by bloody train.'

The radio came to life once more. I began to write down the incoming signal while Jock made tea. He took a mug of the brew into the officer and then wandered off back to the billet.

The signals officer did not emerge from his office until around midnight.

'Not much I can tell you, Chas,' he said when asked what was happening, 'except that we are shortly to expect the arrival of a high ranking officer; an Air Vice Marshal no less.'

The signals officer remained cool and relaxed. He was new to this posting and always addressed his men by first names. They would reciprocate with this informal gesture when he was off-duty and not in uniform, otherwise 'Sir' was used as a mark of respect for his commission.

The officer prepared to leave but before he went, he instructed, 'If a top secret priority signal comes through during the night phone me at once, please.'

I sat pondering over his last remarks. This was a complete break in routine. But in spite of the expectations that had been built up things remained quiet. The night passed by without a bleep.

The following days were very much in keeping with what was usual except that even when off duty everyone would visit the radio shack in the hope of learning more about the contents of the coded messages.

'Bloody top brass visiting, that's all there is to it,' Paddy speculated. 'No doubt we'll all have to bull up the camp, paint everything in bloody sight and polish a few palm trees.'

'Perhaps World War 3 is about to start,' Brum commented dryly.

Another series of secret coded messages was received a few days later. One of these confirmed the visit of the Air Vice Marshall. He was due to arrive within the coming week.

'There's something funny about this,' Brum stated upon hearing the news. 'Most other stations would at least have a parade for visiting top brass. No doubt we'll find out what it's all about soon.'

Rumours, by their very nature, can be twisted and distorted as they are passed around but those brought back from the airfield that evening were quite straight forward. They came from one of the airmen who worked at the airfield. He came over to join me for a drink in the crowded bar, 'What's going on, Chas? You're in Signals; you must know what's happening.'

I drained my can of beer and replied, 'Why do you ask? What's supposed to be going on?'

'Saw a couple of Yanks get off the Hastybird, today. They went off sniffing around Main Camp with note books in their hands. Later some more arrived in their own kite.'

This news came as a complete surprise to me but I determined not to let it show, 'How nice, perhaps they are wishing to exchange their leave centre from Hawaii over to here. This would be a pleasant spot for them.'

'Come on Chas, you must know something,' he insisted.

I ordered another beer and replied, 'Look mate, all the important signals arrive in code and we don't get to see them all. The only thing that I can tell you is that a bigwig is due to arrive any day now.'

'We all know that!' He sounded disappointed. 'He arrives tomorrow morning.'

This also came as a surprise and I asked, 'How do you know that?'

'I do happen to work in air traffic control.'

It was left at that and I hurried off to tell the others this latest news. The three who were off duty went immediately to the radio cabin to see if there was any more information.

Signals traffic had again been heavy that evening. Brum was getting writer's cramp so help was given to clear the backlog of messages to be sent out. Confirmation of the Air Vice Marshal's arrival was in hand. There was also an announcement that he would be addressing all personnel the following evening in the camp cinema.

'Probably going to tell us that we can all go home because they've given the place to the Yanks,' Paddy stated.

'World War 3,' Brum echoed blackly, 'Told you so.'

On the next day, for the first time since arriving on the island, the radio shack was officially closed down for an hour to enable all to attend the meeting. Officers and men of the three services crowded into the small open-air cinema shortly before the arrival of the Air Vice Marshal. When he entered the excited chatter ceased abruptly.

He took up a position on the platform, in front of the screen. He began the address along these lines, 'Good evening everyone. This is the first time that I have had the pleasure of paying a visit to this delightful little island of yours.'

He scanned the rows of men in front of him as he spoke.

'I must say, you all look rather healthy for it.'

Mock laughter rippled through his audience.

'I am here to inform you that over the next few weeks, the strength of this station will be increased by 75 or so men. They are to be installed within the existing accommodation, here in the Port Area, which means that most of you will have one or two extra bodies sharing your rooms. At the same time, approximately two and a half thousand American servicemen will be moving into Main Camp near the airfield.

'It all adds up to this; the Americans will be conducting a series of thermo-nuclear tests which will commence towards the end of April. The thermo-nuclear device, or H-Bomb as it is commonly known, will be detonated above the sea off the island. We are not sure at this point how many tests are to be carried out but you will be informed about things as, and when, necessary.

'This nuclear test programme has been named Operation Dominic by the Americans. For our part, it is called Brigadoon. The maintaining of security around these operations is of paramount importance and you will be informed, to this end, over the coming weeks. You may take photographs of the tests but not cine film. Anyone caught taking moving pictures will have their cameras confiscated and disciplinary action taken against them. Moving film would reveal too much information about the nature of each test.

'To give you a rough idea of what to expect, we are now going to show a film that was taken during the 1950s tests on the island, known as Operation Grapple.'

As he stepped from the platform, nothing could be heard except the wind blowing gently against the corrugated tin walls of the cinema. This uncanny silence was broken by the whirring of the projector a few moments later.

The film was a well-photographed documentary. It showed the last nuclear bomb tests carried out on the island. For fifteen minutes pictures flashed across the screen of the hydrogen bomb and its violent explosive power. It was explained that in the process of nuclear fusion certain types of hydrogen are transformed into helium. It was learned that this happens at extremely high temperatures where heat is supplied by the detonation of an atomic bomb.

We watched the vivid pictures in an enthralled silence. When the screen flickered white at the end of the film it was as though a signal had been given for everybody to talk at once.

A noisy throng left the cinema, most of them intending to discuss the situation over a beer.

'Bloody Aussie Radio got their dates wrong, didn't they?' someone complained.

'They're going to be big bastards then. It takes an A-Bomb to set off an H-Bomb. They'll all be in the megaton class that's for sure.'

'Why we are getting mixed up with the Yankee tests? You know they fucked up Bikini Atoll with their tests a few years ago.'

Information came thick and fast as people exchanged knowledge acquired mainly from past journals and newspaper reports. Bikini Atoll between 1954 and 1958 was the main topic of conversation. One of the first bombs exploded there, by the Americans, was a 15 megaton H-bomb. It was on Bikini that radioactive fallout from one explosion had descended from a cloud, over a 100,000 feet high, and had unexpectedly spread radioactive dust across one end of the island. It also contaminated Rongelap, a nearby atoll, as well as a Japanese fishing vessel. The inhabitants of Rongelap had remained under medical supervision.

'In other words you end up as bloody guinea pigs,' someone muttered. 'What happened to the so-called suspension of atmospheric tests?'

He was given the answer that the Russians tests had started again; between September and October 1961, thirty bombs had been detonated in Russia, including a 60 megaton one. It was now the American's turn.

'It's like a game of chess and we're in for the Yank's move. Christ! Are we in for that many?'

'Why should we get involved in their game? We're pawns that shouldn't be on the bloody board.'

Jock had said very little. He was tightened into an uneasy scowl which simmered slowly over a few uneasy beers until he growled, 'Fairy tale time. Brigadoon - huh!'

He spoke to himself rather than to us but curiosity to know what he was mumbling about surfaced, 'What's the matter with calling it that? Operation Brigadoon sounds just up your street, Jock. Something to do with the clans is it?'

Without moving his head, he gave me an exasperated look but answered patiently, 'Brigadoon is the story of a magical Scottish village. Appearing from nowhere; it comes to life every now and then.'

'Glad to know that one of them does,' interrupted Brum. 'Is that when the whisky runs out?'

Jock ignored him, 'An interesting thing to think about, Charlie. Imagine, the whole world has become a radioactive grave by the end of the century. Brigadoon begins to appear slowly through the mists of time and...'

'Shit! No Scots!' Brum finished for him. 'Just lochs glowing in the dark. That'll be a disappointment for them, won't it? They won't take kindly to you helping to bring it about, will they?'

'Aye, but it's a liberty with the name all the same,' Jock smiled. 'Especially when you think that Brigadoon is about places which disappear off the face of the earth!'

Brum turned his attention away from Brigadoon, 'I'll be away from this island before they start testing, mid - April at the latest.'

'You'll miss all the fun. Fancy being here for a year and then having to miss the fireworks party.'

'Strangely enough, I'd like to stay,' he said.

'You sound serious. Be careful, we might believe you.'

'You know,' he insisted. 'There will probably never be another chance to see an H-bomb go off unless there is a major war. I wouldn't mind staying to see a few.'

'Tell you what I'll take your flight home, if you like.'

'No chance,' he sounded definite. 'I'm not that bloody curious.'

CHAPTER NINE

Enter Mahatma

Within a month of the Air Vice Marshal's talk in the cinema a plane load of British servicemen arrived from the UK. They were given the customary greeting and allocated their quarters. The extra beds in our room were to accommodate two airmen who would be working in communications.

The cheery curly headed corporal with a Suez decoration over his shirt pocket, put his kit-bag on top of one of the spare beds.

'Name's John.'

We shook hands and introduced ourselves.

'Where are you from?'

'Middlesex. What a greeting! When I stepped off the bus and saw that screaming bunch, I thought it was Custer's Last Stand all over again.'

The other airman was younger than John. He flopped down on to a spare bed and with a wave said, 'Call me Rocky.'

He had a London accent and was extremely sure of himself.

'Is that your real name?' Brum enquired.

'No, but it sounds good, don't it?'

'We need more comedians round here,' said Brum unconvincingly.

'Name's Bill really,' the Londoner finally admitted.

John began unpacking his kit. He recounted that he had been given a fortnight's notice that he was to be posted and thought that he was being sent to the Far East for three months. He had only been given correct information about his destination, and the reason for it, just before he left, when everyone was assembled at Gloucester.

Bill, alias Rocky, had now put his suitcase on the bed to begin unpacking. 'This is the first time I've ever been abroad. It's my first posting.'

'Boy entrant?'

'Yeah, that's right.'

'That makes two of you. You'll meet young Paddy when he comes off shift.'

'I can't wait,' he said unenthusiastically.

'You'll have to.'

After one or two weeks the new arrivals had settled in. They quickly became acquainted with their duties and with the facilities that the Port Camp offered. Bill, the young Londoner, settled in faster than anyone. He was attracted by the idea of weight-lifting and had visions of returning to the UK, looking like Charles Atlas sporting a golden tan. He had a clear idea in his mind of how he would like to impress his girlfriend when he got home. Together, we decided to pay a visit to Muscle Beach.

We were the only two present and the Station Warrant Officer gave his undivided attention. He put us through the paces for more than an hour. He was an extremely well built and healthy looking man for his fifty-odd years but he had a way with him that was no less than comic.

'Right, lads, we're not weight-lifting but weight-training. Remember that. Don't want to bust a gut, pull a muscle or bleedin' rupture yourselves, do you?'

'No chief,' we chorused.

'Use that bar-bell with fifty pounds on it, 25 pounds on each end to start with and in a few weeks you'll be training with 250 pounds, like myself.'

He demonstrated a simple exercise, which entailed raising the weighted bar, from the waist-high stand, to the chin, then from the chin to above the head, as far as outstretched arms would allow.

We were exhausted after a while but the Warrant Officer was still going strong and continued to talk the whole time.

'It'll come, lads. It'll come. Got to take care in building up the old muscles.'

The sweat was pouring off him in some profusion as he continued the exercise. I congratulated myself on having the good sense to bring a towel to mop up the perspiration which was running into my eyes. I noticed that he was suffering from the same problem; his eyes were screwed up. They were, no doubt, stinging painfully, as mine were.

Upon finishing his exercises, the Warrant Officer made an effort to place the bar-bell on the stand. He misjudged the position and the weight came crashing down.

After mumbling a stream of gentle oaths, he assured us, 'Just grazed my shin. Got to be careful. Just shows you what can happen.'

We managed to stifle a smile. The remark had been made in such a way that the casual observer would think the accident was engineered for our benefit instead of being caused by the failure to comply with his own safety rules.

After a few days, I lost interest in weight-training and it was not too long after this that the Warrant Officer was seen wearing a sling on his right arm. Nothing much had happened during this period of time. The new British arrivals settled in but it was reported that Main Camp was showing very little sign of life.

Late one morning, even more hot and humid than usual, Paddy was with me on duty in the WT shack. Not much air was coming through the louvre windows. What little breeze there was did nothing to alleviate the sweating stickiness of the place. The small room was lifelessly hot and quiet apart from the endless whirr of the ceiling fan.

Suddenly the lethargy of the place was interrupted. The ship-to-shore radio boomed into life. The voice which reverberated from the speaker was much louder than usual. The caller vibrated from the radio with an unmistakenly American drawl. He was using one of our call signs and was now asking, 'How do you copy? Over.'

I picked up the microphone and replied, 'Loud and clear. Strength five. Anything for us?'

There was a pause, as though the voice at the other end was taking things in for a second or as though he had been surprised by an unfamiliar accent.

During the pause, I turned to Paddy and said, 'Well, that's it! Peace and quiet over, the Yanks are here.'

The American voice completed its official message, then asked, 'You fellas wanna come aboard for lunch with us?'

'If we can get a lift in a tender. You're on.'

'No problem,' the voice boomed and crackled. 'One of ours is going back and forth to your Port jetty all the time. When you get to the ship, I'll be at the unloading bay. Over.'

'We finish at midday. Hope to see you around 1300 hours. Over and out.'

The end of the morning came and we made our way to the jetty. It had become littered with large wooden crates and oil drums. The smell of diesel fuel wafted in the air. With the aid of derricks, American sailors were quickly and energetically unloading cargo from their tender. Two trucks stood nearby. Goods and equipment destined for Main Camp were being loaded into the trucks by American airmen. They wore neatly pressed shirts and trousers. Old-fashioned forage caps, worn in a tilted fashion to one side of the head completed a stylish uniform which did them credit. Crumpled shirts, worn leather sandals and tatty-looking bush hats, which had only been put on to mark the occasion of the visit, were no match for this.

'Been a whole lot better, if we'd just worn shorts and sandals,' Paddy observed.

But, on further consideration, we decided that it was probably etiquette that we should turn up in some kind of recognizable uniform when visiting a foreign ship.

We walked along the wooden jetty towards a sailor from one of the American tenders who looked like the coxswain. He agreed to take us to the ship, the *Monticello*, and said that he would be leaving in about five minutes. When the unloading was complete, he wasted no time in getting his crew aboard and the boat ready to leave.

The diesel engines throbbed gently and pushed the boat away from the jetty and out into the lagoon. It moved towards the thin white line of foam which marked the reef. Crossing the reef was reminiscent of a ride on a big dipper at the fair; a sensation that churned the stomach and legs as the small ship plunged and rose on the white waves. There was no glimpse of the wall of coral below, only a seething blanket of froth on the water's surface. Immediately the ship had crossed the reef it was surrounded by a school of dolphins. They dived and plunged, almost in formation, as though they were an official escort to the ship; these fascinating creatures seldom left the sea to enter the shallow waters of the lagoon.

The *Monticello* had looked big from the beach. It was only on getting nearer to the ship that its size could be fully appreciated. It was massive. A huge flap at the stern lay open to the sea and other tenders could be seen neatly parked inside. Our craft bobbed up and down as it heaved to against the side. A door opened at the same level and we stepped aboard without any inconvenience.

The wireless operator was there to greet us.

'Hi! Glad you could make it. I'm Rick.'

We shook hands and introduced ourselves.

'We've gotta long walk to the mess. It's a couple of decks above us. Follow me.'

89

His accent betrayed a slight drawl characteristic of the southern states of America. Over an excellent lunch Rick told us that he had never met anyone from Britain before.

'Which part of The States do you come from?' Paddy enquired.

'North Carolina.'

'That's on the Atlantic coast, isn't it?'

'You got it. I live about twenty miles from the most beautiful beaches.'

We continued to exchange information about ourselves together with views and opinions although the pending H-Bomb tests did not enter the conversation.

One of Rick's shipmates suggested an exchange of coins as a memento of the visit. We dug into pockets and produced a handful of coins. He picked up a penny and examined it closely. He then held it aloft.

He remarked, 'Hell! Would you believe it? This is a 1959 penny? If it's that size, how big are the coins worth more? The bigger our coins are, the more they are worth.'

The lack of American knowledge about things outside the United States always came as a surprise. I wondered if this good-natured sailor had really sailed the Seven Seas. I wished it were possible to conjure up a dustbin lid and try to pass it off as a half-crown to pretend a greater logic to our system of currency. As it was, a real half-crown was pointed out to them and we admitted that this was the largest denomination of our coins in general circulation although only about the same size as the penny.

Rick then conducted a tour of the ship. At least, we were shown part of the ship; it was too large to see it all in the few hours there were to spend before returning. Everywhere we went there was a welcoming hospitality but that was not the thing which filled us with regret when the time came to board the tender for the return journey to the jetty. It was the thought of going back to the island that was uppermost in our minds. And, sure enough, stepping onto land at Port Camp was like being a long-marooned mariner who having reached a ship found himself being courteously returned to the torment of his desert island.

The American presence quickly became more obvious on the island. We did not have to wait long before further contact with them in the Port Camp area. It was the next evening when four US airmen pulled up in a jeep and parked outside the NAAFI.

'Can a guy get a drink around here?' they drawled.

'Make yourselves at home.'

'You guys join us?' We nodded assent and ordered six cans of Red Barrel. We asked how many of them were at Main Camp.

'Only a handful. A couple of dozen, maybe,' one of them informed us.

'Are you lot sorting the place out?'

'Hell, no. Civilian contractors come in and do all that. I guess they're about due out tomorrow. The job will be done in a week or so. Our guys will move in after that.'

'I see you get a company car with your job,' Jock observed.

'You might say that. It's kinda funny, though, having to drive on the wrong side of the road.' He managed to sound totally convinced that the American way is the right way. This was to cause some Americans great difficulty during their stay on the island. Jock took a sip of beer and glanced at me before he replied, 'Well, you'll be all right here, if you do keep to the left, because everybody else does.'

At this point, Brum came over to the bar. He had come to celebrate. He had just finished his last shift and would be leaving on the following day. He was looking very pleased with himself both because he was going home and because this posting allowed the planning of a route back to the UK. He had carefully worked out an interesting itinerary for the homeward journey. He had with him confirmation of his repatriation as well as the approval of his planned routing.

He discussed his destinations with the Americans and finally read out to us, 'Hastybird to Hawaii, a Boeing 707 to Los Angeles, overland express train to Arizona for a week's stay. I've always wanted to be in cowboy country, train to New York and finally New York to Heathrow.'

'That's enough, you're depressing me.'

'You're turn will come, eventually.'

'As long as we don't get blown there by bomb blast.'

Just before he left Brum managed to collect a little spending money for the journey home. He used the wily old ginger tom, who had been adopted by our block, for the purpose. Brum organised a sweep concerning the cat. He asked Paddy and me if we wanted to enter, at sixpence a go.

'What's it all about?' I asked.

'It's the ginger tom. He's cornering a black and white female.'

'You've got to be kidding!'

'No, seriously, done it before some six months back. Just put your name down with the time you reckon it's going to take (minutes, seconds or whatever). It's timed from when the tom gets hold of her by the scruff of the neck.'

We hurried outside to join the group of men that surrounded the pair of felines. People were putting their names down and handing over sixpences to the holder of the stakes, who was Brum's partner in this enterprise.

'Now I've seen it all,' Paddy commented with some disbelief.

'It hasn't started yet,' Brum answered with a laugh.

Suddenly the ginger tom grabbed hold of the queen by the scruff of her neck and a stop watch was set in motion.

Men cheered and made side bets as the female sat on her haunches. The tom crouched directly behind his mate and waited patiently for her to rise. Within a frantic five minutes or so it was all over. Times had been checked and money handed over to the winner.

'How much was in the kitty?' Paddy enquired, innocently.

Brum eyed the cats thoughtfully for a moment before he looked up and replied, with a devilish grin, 'There's no way of telling, is there, really?'

I wondered whether he would stop off at Las Vegas. Brum's sardonic and humorous company was to be missed. He would have been an asset during the days when the shadow of the bombs were to loom miserably over this god-forsaken place.

It was at this point that even though there was frantic activity going on in other parts of the island things became very quiet in the billet. Not only did we say goodbye to Brum but Jock went to Hawaii to take his leave before the tests. When he returned he had a tale to tell 'Wore ma kilt in Hawaii.'

'Did it help you get your end away, Jock?' asked Bill, cheekily.

'Nearly, very nearly,' Jock replied. Bill's question acted as a cue for Jock to recount some of his past week's experiences. Bill listened avidly.

Amongst the memories, was the night that Jock had been drinking in the American NCO's club. The events of this night were etched deeply into his mind. It all began when he was lounging, nonchalantly and innocently, at the bar and a woman danced very close to him. She had long red hair. She was wearing a deep red and black dress. He could smell her perfume. The dress clung to a beautifully shaped body that moved voluptuously to the rhythm of the cha-cha and he thought it was fascinating how her skirt gently lifted, with her swaying hips, to reveal her tanned and shapely legs.

He could not help but watch her through the next few dances. She met his eyes with a sultry look, as he hungrily followed her movements. Jock knew that American woman were often very forward and that this one could have been leading him on a little. Even so he was, by this time, far from sober and he fancied his chances with the beautiful red-head. Towards the end of the evening he was dancing with her. He felt the smooth arms against the back of his neck and he experienced the warmth of the curved body.

She was not loud when she spoke, like some American women, but soft and coy. She told him she was married to a Sergeant and introduced him to some of the people she had come with. They all continued drinking until late. Every time she got up to dance with any of her friends he sat watching her longingly. Jock was very much the worse for wear when one of the men asked him what he thought of their lady.

'Well I can tell you this,' he slurred. 'After being on that rock, thousands of miles from anywhere, without hardly sight of a woman for seven months, I can tell you how I feel. At this very moment I'd really like to shaft her, that's a fact.'

He was not sure of the reason for what happened next. He felt it could have been a case of a misunderstanding of the Scottish brogue; the Americans, perhaps, just did not understand British slang. Maybe he should have reckoned on the American's creative ability and willingness to comply with any request. Before he realized what was happening he was being helped into a car.

He was sped through the night until he was vaguely aware that he was at some kind of military establishment. The car gradually slowed down as it reached the entrance. Through a haze of tiredness and drink he caught sight of the sign as the vehicle moved slowly into the camp. He could not believe what he saw. The notice read, 'FORT

SHAFTER'.

He had no idea where he was when he woke up the next morning. He quickly realized he had no shoes, or wallet or ID card. Suddenly the door opened and an American military policeman stood in front of him and called out his name.

'Is that your name?'

'Aye,' said Jock wondering what was going to happen to him next.

At this point in telling the story, he paused. This caused Bill to say, 'Well go on. What happened next?'

'Would you believe there is a Fort Shafter on Hawaii? The MP verified that's where I was,' said Jock. 'Then he handed me my belongings. He had never seen a Scotsman in a kilt before and he was quite taken aback. You know what I'm like after a period of suspended animation. I must have looked as though I'd come straight out of the hills, all wild and woolly like. Anyway he ended up saluting me.'

'Salute anything the Yanks will,' Bill commented dryly.

'So,' Jock continued. 'That was that.'

'Had a good time then.' I said.

'Oh, aye. Aye.'

By the time Jock had returned from Hawaii. Main Camp had become re-established with its full complement of men. The main road connecting with Port Camp began to support more traffic. It was easy to hitch a lift from a passing jeep, Land Rover or truck. This did much to enhance the life of those staying in the Port Area.

'Fancy a trip to America's fifty-first state, Jock?'

'What's that Charles?'

'Main Camp. How about paying it a visit? Plenty of wheelies going up and down the road now. It's getting like the M1 motorway.'

'Why not, it'll save vegetating here for another afternoon.'

'Better wear a shirt and take a hat - some kind of uniform. Don't want to get shot as spies.'

The driver of the jeep was on his way to the airfield. He dropped us off, conveniently, at the entrance to Main Camp. We walked through the open gates and made our way down a road that led to the centre of the camp.

Main Camp had come to life with a vengeance. Brigadoon it was. Almost as though from nowhere, with unbelievable energy, it had appeared from the deserted ghost town. It now looked like a bustling, thriving centre; a million-dollar complex. There was an open air cinema, many times larger than the one at Port Camp. Behind the low wall of the cinema were rows of tiered seats. Entrance was free and different films were shown every night. The Base Exchange was their equivalent to our NAAFI shop and it was from there that we discovered where the nearest bar was located. It was called the Surf Club.

Once inside the club, acquaintance with some of its inhabitants was rapid. They were a friendly lot and eager to converse.

'So you guys are from Port Camp?'

'Yes, it's a lot smaller than this one. Come down there some time. What's your accommodation like?' Jock asked them.

'Mostly two or three to a room. Say, I'm going back to mine right now; you guys follow me and I'll show you.'

Their room, although more compact than ours, had an air of luxury about it. We glanced with envy at the interior sprung mattresses and thought of our hard flock-filled bedding. But the thing that was beyond belief and which had pride of place was a full-size refrigerator. Our host walked up to the refrigerator and opened its door. It was stacked out, bursting with cans of beer.

'Here, catch!' Two cans were tossed in our direction.

'We could do with a fridge, like that, down at our end,' I remarked as I sipped the refreshingly ice-cool beer.

'Oh, you mean the ice-box. Ain't you got one?'

'They don't exist in the Port area. If there is one in the NAAFI bar, it must be an ornament because our beer is never served cold.'

'So you guys wanna ice box. I think I may know where there's a spare one lying around.'

'Are you kidding?'

'Course not. Let's go find it.'

He led the way to a row of empty rooms and pushed open one of the unlocked doors. A brand new refrigerator stood in a corner of an unoccupied room.

'There you go, one ice box. Here I'll give you a hand to get it out.'

He helped to remove it from the room then said, 'Well, I've gotta go on duty right now, so I'll see you guys around sometime.'

'Thanks a lot.'

'Don't mention it.'

Jock and I managed to carry the cumbersome fridge to the road that led to the entrance of the camp. We stopped to catch our breath and Jock straightened up for a moment.

'Do you think that Yank was authorized to give us this fridge Charlie? He doesn't look the sort of fellow that would drop you in the shit but in this case I'd say that it's easier to give than to receive.'

Just then a small truck pulled up beside us and an American Sergeant jumped out. He asked where we were taking our load. Hearts sank. Immediate thoughts were that not only would we be deprived of the fridge but, worse of all, we could end up in trouble.

I tried not to sound guilty and boldly stated, 'Port Camp, Sergeant.'

'I'm going down there right now. Here, let me give you a hand - there's plenty of room at the back.'

Jock and I looked at each other, hardly believing our good fortune.

'That's very nice of you, Sergeant. It's going to the communications centre.'

He lowered the tailgate and the three of us heaved the heavy refrigerator on board. As we climbed into the truck, we asked him if he had ever been to Port Camp before.

'Only a couple of times. Seems to be a lot of to-ing and fro-ing all the time.'

Anxious to keep off the subject of movement between the camps, Jock asked him whether he liked the island.

'I've been here three weeks. I already feel that's enough. No damn broads here, that's the trouble.'

The truck came to a halt outside the WT shack. The Sergeant helped to unload the ice-box then left us, standing triumphant at the door with our prized possession.

Paddy was the first to come out to see the new acquisition, 'What have you got there?'

'I would say it's something that resembles a fridge,' Jock replied.

'Big enough, isn't it?'

'They had sold out of the economy model.'

Paddy walked around the refrigerator looking it up and down.

'How did you come by it?' he asked.

'Without going into too much detail, let's just say that it has been redeployed from Main Camp.'

'In other words, you've nicked it.'

'Not in so many words. Come on, give us a hand to get it inside.'

Before the day was over, the refrigerator had been admired by all who worked in the radio cabin. The Section Officer was as excited about it as anybody else. We had recently discovered that his father was a Member of

Parliament back home in England and we thought perhaps that his enthusiasm was due to the fact that he was used to wining and dining in style. Jock and I succeeded in avoiding a direct answer to the question of exactly how it came into our hands. We thought it might be a grey area.

The next item on the agenda was stocking it out. There had already been total confusion among the catering staff when they first had to cope with the innovation of drawing raw rations. Now perishable commodities could be added to the supply of food in the radio cabin.

Within a week the huge fridge had been stocked out with dozens of eggs, bacon, beer, cans of corned beef and anything edible or drinkable that could be got from the muddled catering staff. A mixing bowl was obtained to help develop latent culinary skills and soon such dishes as pancakes could be attempted to vary the menu. The small electric ring now seemed somewhat inadequate for our needs and we felt that we could do with better facilities.

Our interest in food now almost became an obsession, so that when an airfield worker mentioned in casual conversation that he had eaten in the American airmen's mess, this was pounced on at once and he was thoroughly cross-examined on every detail. The airman said that he had found the food first rate. We decided to go and sample it immediately.

That evening we made our way to Main Camp once more. The airfield worker had warned that there would be a queue outside the American airmen's mess because the doors did not open before six o'clock. However the long line of men waiting outside made my jaw drop. I began to wonder whether the idea of sampling their food had been a good one.

A bell rang out at the appointed hour and the doors were flung wide open. The line of men moved so fast that we entered the building almost trotting. Inside were rows upon rows of neatly laid tables complete with plates and platters of food.

Jock and I sat opposite each other at a table for eight. Eager hands moved in all directions, filling plates to the brim. It was as though it was the last meal that they would ever get. One overweight airman finished off a plate of steaks before I had the chance to get one. Another airman, sitting opposite, held the empty dish aloft and, within half a minute, it was replaced with a fresh plate-full.

'This is more like it,' said Jock, in between mouthfuls. Then leaning across the table to avoid being heard, 'No wonder they look so flabby! They must stuff themselves silly if every meal is like this one.'

At the end of the dinner, pots of coffee were placed on the table. The fat American leaned back in his chair and lit a huge cigar. He then looked at us as though he had only just realized that he was not alone at the table. This was hardly surprising because the amount of food that he had consumed would have taken precedence over and above anything else.

Blowing a large cloud of smoke towards the ceiling, he said, 'How long you guys been living on this coral shit?'

'Nearly five months,' I replied and nodded towards Jock. 'Jock's been here nigh on eight months.'

'Jesus! Whad ya do wrong? Rob a bank or something?'

It was send-up time. Keeping a serious look on my face, I replied, 'No nothing like that. You see we are, what you might say, indispensable to certain operations on the island. We like it here and will probably stay here for another three or four years.'

Jock nearly choked on his coffee. The American looked as though he was only half convinced, 'Say, you guys are putting me on, aren't you?'

He began chewing on his cigar and his chubby face broke into a wide grin.

'Say, I haven't met any Britishers before. You're Scotch aren't you?' he said looking at Jock.

'I'm not a bloody drink. Scotch is a whisky. I am Scots.'

'Well whadya know,' he mused, turning his attention to me.

'I'm English,' I volunteered in as disdainful a manner as I could muster wanting to laugh. 'What part of the North American Colonies are you from?'

Keeping his composure and looking uncertain about the seriousness of the question, he replied, 'Gee, I heard something of the British being quaint but I didn't realize until just now what that meant.'

We broke into laughter.

'Say, you guys are all right. Come on. I'll buy you a beer.'

A couple of beers, and a king-sized cigar later, he introduced us to their gambling tent which turned out to be a medium sized marquee. The sounds of snapping cards, rolling dice, roulette wheels clicking and voices filled with disappointment and glee, could be heard on the approach to the entrance.

Inside through the smoky haze a cigar-butt chewing airman was scooping up 500 dollars, at the Black Jack table, only to lose it all after a further five minutes on so called good hands.

'You wanna play?' our host enquired.

'No thanks. I've taken the cure.'

'How about bingo? Game starts in about fifteen minutes. Costs two dollars, 75 dollar wins. Jackpot's over 700, depends how many are playing or how many cards they buy.'

The Jackpot turned out to be 750 dollars. It was won by someone we recognized as one of our own airmen from the Port Camp fire station. There were cries of 'Asshole! Asshole!' from the losers followed by the screwing up of cards and tossing them at the caller. We were now of the firm opinion that life on this camp was very different from our own.

After that evening we became regular visitors to Main Camp. On subsequent visits we were given interior sprung mattresses and soon the whole billet could sleep in comfort. On another occasion we were also handed a large electric grill that had been discarded to make room for new equipment. Along the way we had managed to acquire plates and extra cutlery and the WT shack gradually took on the appearance of a well-run cafe. So much so that the shack became a regular stopping place in the evening for any of us who were off duty and guests. It was suggested that we were dining better than some of the officers and this was supported by their occasional presence at supper time.

Meanwhile the word about the Main Camp mess spread fast. Numbers attending the evening meal at the British mess were becoming severely depleted. It had to happen. Orders were given to take place immediately; personnel from Port Camp would not be admitted to the Main Camp mess hall unless they were working in the area at the time. That was it. It was good while it lasted. We in Signals were not too bothered for we had well and truly established our own deluxe catering system.

With the interest in food becoming increasingly obsessive it was not long before it became necessary to combat the self indulgence of the food supply. I resolved to take up weight training once more and to pay Muscle Beach another visit.

It was midday and I quickly discovered why the place was always deserted at this time. The barbells were so hot that it was impossible to handle them. I made one or two half-hearted attempts to pick them up and then abandoned the idea of exercise for the moment. I was about to leave when the Warrant Officer approached. He was busily pulling some gloves onto his hands. His thigh was bandaged.

'Pulled a muscle, chief?'

'No, son. A spot of gunge, that's all, a spot of gunge. You just arrived or are you leaving?'

'I've had enough for one day chief. I'm just off.'

'You must have hands like bleeding leather,' he mumbled.

I left him puffing and grunting and made my way over to the communications hut to get a cool beer.

On the way back to the hut, there were two Americans sited by a telegraph pole. They were holding tools and were surrounded by wire. One of them was perched halfway up the pole and was attempting to attach a tannoy loud speaker to it. I wondered what was happening.

'Good afternoon. Want a hand?' I said, trying to sound sincere.

'Hi there,' came the response. 'It's O.K. We're doing just fine. Thanks all the same.'

'What are you doing?'

'Oh, we're just fitting up a public address system around the populated areas of the island so that everybody gets to know what's happening.'

'Good idea,' I commented unnecessarily, and continued the journey back.

John and Bill were busy taking down incoming signals at the cabin. I plucked an ice-cold beer from the fridge, waited for them to finish and then told them about the tannoys.

'It's getting like Butlins Holiday Camp,' John complained.

'Yeah,' Bill added. 'Good morning campers - rise and shine. Today's fun starts with one helluva bang. Just the place for an all-over, all-through sun and radiation tan. Overweight? Enjoy a spot of this weeks special. Instant vaporization.' Bill looked suitably vaporized.

I looked at his hunched form and added, 'It'll make you the shadow of the man you werc.'

John became serious in the midst of our laughter, 'Do you know how many are going to be tested? Twenty odd. Plus one or two in the Van Allen Belt.'

He pushed a week-old newspaper in my direction. It was one that had been recently received from the UK. It contained an article proclaiming that, despite international pressure, the USA was going ahead with nuclear tests on Christmas Island.

'Seems as though the Gilbos might be taken off the island though,' John added. 'They might be put on ships during the tests.'

It was good to know that the Gilbertese, if nobody else, would be given an escape route.

That night was exceptionally warm and humid. Slumped in a chair, with chin resting on chest, I tried to get some sleep. It was in vain. Irregular, staccato bleeps of morse-code frequently filled the room and were like invisible strings pulling me back to life. At the end of the shift, I was very tired and I made welcome retreat to bed. With head nestled firmly into the feather pillow, the sounds of morse-code gradually began to fade into oblivion.

Suddenly the invisible strings were at it again, 'This is Mahatma. This is Mahatma. Testing one, two, three.'

I sat bolt upright and looked out of the window. I could see my tormentor attached to a pole opposite our room.

'This is Mahatma. This is Mahatma. Testing one, two, three.'

Paddy wandered through the door. He was not looking where he was going. His head was turned in continuous observation of the loud speakers.

'Who the bloody hell is Mahatma, when he's out? I thought Gandhi was assassinated years ago.'

'Doesn't sound as though they made a very thorough job of it!' I replied morosely.

The tannoy had injected sudden life and noise everywhere and it was impossible to sleep. I felt annoyed at the intrusion into my relaxed, dazed state and abandoned all hope of getting any further rest. I dressed and left the room. Once outside, I walked up to the American technician who was making some adjustments to the tannoy.

'Morning. Why the Mahatma call-sign? Anything to do with Gandhi?'

'Hell, no. It's supposed to mean someone, or something, with superhuman powers,' smiled back the well-informed technician. He remained smiling at the disgruntled reply.

'Well, it's certainly got enough power to keep us awake.'

I walked off towards the bondi between the large lagoon and the beach. Here it was peaceful. It was a wide stretch of bay bordered by palm trees of all shapes and sizes. Some of the tree-tops were lop-sided; leaves had grown to one side only because of the continual battering from the constant wind. It had made them take on the shape of a child's windmill. I made a nest out of low-hanging palm leaves and settled down in the shade. The gentle rhythmic sounds of the surf caressing the pale sand gradually lulled me into semi-sleep. I day dreamed of home.

Jacky had kept our old cine-camera at home and regularly sent back film of our daughter, Corinne, growing up. The last one had shown the baby crawling about in the garden, through long green grass beside yellow spring daffodils. Everyone in the billet had seen the film two or three times. We had sat contemplating the greenness and springtime of home. Corinne's mischievous face as she posed, momentarily, to look into the camera, had stayed in my mind. I was lulled, along with the waves, back into a different world.

My thoughts were shattered by a voice which pulled me back with an instant shock.

'This is Mahatma. This is Mahatma. Testing one, two, three.'

'Hell!' I thought aloud. 'They've even got the bloody tannoys in the palm trees!'

CHAPTER TEN

Megaton morning

The Section Warrant Officer came into the WT shack carrying a cardboard box. He placed it on the end of the workbench and said briskly, 'Right, help yourselves to goggles and a film radiation badge.'

I pulled a pair of black-lensed goggles from amongst the tangle of others in the box and held them up to the afternoon sun which shone blindingly through the window. Through the black lenses the sun's luminosity was almost extinguished and it took on the appearance of a dull grey moon. The radiation badge, that was to adorn our suntanned necks resembled a small, light grey tablet of soap. It was rectangular in shape and measured two inches by one and a half inches.

After the Warrant Officer had left, we sat at the bench examining the new acquisitions. We turned the unimpressive looking badges over in our hands repeatedly, scanning them closely for clues on how they functioned.

'What's supposed to happen to these things if anybody gets exposed to too much radiation, then?' Paddy wondered aloud.

'No idea! If they're made in the US, maybe they start flashing red, white and blue and whistle 'Colonel Bogey'. Who knows?' He diverted his attention to the goggles, 'These glorified sun glasses will be all right to view next month's partial eclipse, don't you think?'

Paddy looked unconvinced. He doubted whether he would be interested in astronomy during the coming month. His one concern was with the idea of being close to the bomb when it was detonated. He was not satisfied with reassurances about precautions which would ensure that fall-out did not drop on the island. He wanted to know how the wind direction was checked.

'Have you noticed how temperamental the wind is here?' he mused suspiciously. 'It blows more than one way simultaneously. You can actually see the clouds crossing each other at different levels.'

'Well, let's hope they really know which way the wind's blowing.' I said cheerfully, trying to camouflage any hint of unease.

The tannoy system was now fully operative throughout the island. There was to be a dummy run on events. This was to take place, using conventional explosives, on 16 April. Soon there was to be a period when Mahatma would persistently intrude into our lives. This was to be a time when it would be easy to become almost punch-drunk with the constant urging from the tannoy. It started two days before the TNT detonation. There followed further tannoy announcements, throughout the next day and, as the time drew ever closer to the dummy run, Mahatma came with increasing frequency.

During this time, the flies in the camp seemed, for some reason, to double their population overnight. They swarmed around the entrance of the mess hall and crawled and hovered over the tables as the men ate. Captain Flit flew in to alleviate the situation. He appeared, heralded by his distant drone, and swooped over the camp with the ha-bitual white fan of spray following in his wake. Paddy looked glum as he watched people dashing about closing the door and windows.

'They're gonna get us one way or another you know. If it's not bloody DDT, it'll be fallout.'

Jock thought he would cheer him up by saying that evacuation procedures had been posted up in the radio cabin that morning. If anything went wrong the men in the Port area would embark on one of the ships beyond the reef.

'Lotta use that'll be,' argued Paddy. 'It takes at least three quarters of an hour to get on a ship out there, even with everything in your favour.'

'Well, it would probably take just as long to get to the airfield. So what's the odds?' said Jock, shrugging his shoulders and looking resigned to it all.

On the day of the dummy run, the tannoy woke the camp early. Everyone in the billet crowded outside, just before the prescribed half hour, to listen to the explosion. But the only sound after the TNT detonation was a low rumble, reminiscent of distant thunder. It was not much of a noise. This rehearsal prelude was not really a sample of what was to come.

Easter was near and the next Friday was Good Friday. Orders had been posted around the camp warning about the contents of any letters sent home. Should anything be leaked personal correspondence would be censored. The countdown would start two days before the first test, D minus two.

It was Saturday 21 April 1962. It seemed strange that Easter Monday had been chosen for the first test. Even for those who were not religious the choice seemed to fly in the face of deeply held beliefs.

As things transpired there was no need for that particular concern. In fact the test did not take place that day. On Easter Sunday, 22 April 1962 the tannoy boomed out that there was a hold in the run. This signified that the test would be delayed and Easter would be left intact. The countdown would re-start on Easter Monday 23 April.

'This is Mahatma. This is Mahatma. D minus two. D minus two.'

It was now Wednesday for the big bang. Orders were given to the effect that all personnel in the Port Area were to assemble on the football pitch half an hour before the bomb was due to be detonated and that all cats and dogs should be locked in the billets.

This countdown continued and did not let up until nightfall, then all fell silent. D minus one commenced the following morning and was followed by hourly announcements until nightfall once again.

At 5.00 am on Wednesday 25 April the countdown started in earnest. The detonation had been scheduled for 6.45 am. Operation Dominic had well and truly commenced.

'This is Mahatma. This is Mahatma. D minus one hour and 45 minutes. D minus one hour and 45 minutes.'

'Don't need an alarm clock with that racket going on out there,' Bill growled as he got out of bed. 'I'm going to take a pillow with me if I'm sitting on that bloody football pitch for any length of time.'

It was dark outside. The sun did not rise on the island before 7.30 am. At 6.15 am, with mugs of tea in hands, we joined the other personnel shuffling their way to the football pitch. The dusty coral appeared ghostly white in the moonless night. The darkness beyond was interrupted by the irregular displacement of electric lamps around the camp and by the starry sky above.

Everyone sat down facing towards the direction of the yachting lagoon. The detonation was to take place some miles beyond this area. With radiation badges about our necks and goggles held in sweaty hands, we chatted idly amongst ourselves, waiting patiently for the appointed time. An empty mug now stood on the ground beside me as a gentle breeze carried wisps of coral sand across the surface of the pitch.

A senior NCO addressed the assembly, 'Right men. At D minus one minute I want everybody to put on their goggles. Do not, I repeat, do not look at the flash without them if you ever want to see again. You may take them off after eight seconds from the initial flash but not before. Is that clear?'

A ripple of assent echoed across the pitch.

'D minus 5 minutes,' the tannoy announced, signifying the time before the bomb was dropped.

By now goggles were being worn on foreheads, in readiness.

'Look like a load of bug-eyed monsters,' Bill remarked. 'Be glad when it's all over and I can get back to bed.'

The countdown continued. Seconds ticked away. I could not believe that it was actually about to happen; that there was nothing I could do about it.

The voice from the tannoy interrupted my chain of thoughts, 'D minus one minute.'

The NCO shouted, 'Right goggles on now.'

The dark glasses rendered me blind; totally blind. The excited chatter ceased abruptly, leaving a sense of feeling alone and completely isolated. The only sound to be heard was that of the coral sand being gently pushed along by the breeze.

This brief, but seemingly eternal moment was shattered with, 'D minus fifty seconds.'

With eyes wide open staring into a black void, I wiped moist palms along the sides of my khaki shorts.

'D minus forty seconds.'

I never realized a minute could be so long. Time expanded with the interminable waiting.

'D minus thirty seconds.'

The voice was ideally suited to the tannoy. It was an unexcited, unemotional, mechanical voice with an American accent.

'D minus twenty seconds.'

The strap on my goggles was adjusted too tight and began to irritate.

'D minus ten seconds, nine, eight, seven, six, five, four, three, two, one. Release!'

The aircraft, a B 52 bomber, which could not be seen from the island, had released its deadly cargo; it had off-loaded the most destructive force yet created by man. The bomb would fall towards the sea for thousands of feet, until it reached the level at which it was to be detonated.

'One minute and fifty seconds to detonation.'

The unseen aircraft had now departed the area and was on its way back to base in America. Out there, in the blackness, the bomb was falling towards the sea.

'One minute to detonation.'

I amused myself with the thought that the bomb might fail to explode; that it might drop into the sea like a damp squib. Then, came notions of what would happen if something went wrong. Would everybody be pulverized into particles and lie instantly intermixed with the coral dust about us? Dark shadows in the pale sand. As before, there was an announcement every ten seconds until the final announcement.

'Nine, eight, seven, six, five, four, three, two, one. Zero!'

The word 'zero' condensed a sentence from the Bible, 'Let there be light. And there was light.' At the word 'zero' a new Sun was born thousands of feet above the sea, beyond the lagoon. It grew from a dot to a sphere, much larger than our Sun, in a fraction of a second. Although it was still night, as far as the eye could see, it was as though it were broad daylight. Everything appeared as normal; blue sky, palm trees flapping in the wind, the turquoise waters in the lagoon rippling towards the beach and even a bird flying in the air. In fact, it was as though goggles were not being worn at all. The only reminder of these were servicemen scattered about the football pitch with large black patches where their eyes should be and bemused looks on their faces. Above them, the bird was now flying aimlessly. It was a creature in the wrong place at the wrong time. It was now condemned to a life of darkness.

The light brought a sensation of warmth; the kind of warmth you might expect from a winter's sun through glass. Within ten seconds the initial flash of light had ebbed and goggles were taken off. It could have been midday. The fireball was expanding continuously and furiously. There was a deadly silence; there was no sound at all, not even a murmur from the men. They sat there as if hypnotized by this awesome, yet somehow wondrous sight. It was as though they were watching the very dawn of creation, while knowing in their hearts that it was a trick, a fraudulent deception and in truth the very essence of destruction itself.

Within ninety seconds the mushroom cloud began to take shape. The incandescent light was now much weaker. It lent the sky the appearance of an artificial sunset. By this time the men were standing and excited voices could be heard reflecting on the events of the past few minutes; as though releasing an inner tension that had been building up for some while.

Then without exception the noise of the blast took everyone by surprise. It was a violent and deafening explosion of sound and vibration. It was a terrifying noise that moved the earth; one that jarred and scraped across every nerve in the body. It came unexpectedly as though some foolhardy clown had crept up and, without warning, had fired both barrels of a shotgun at once. The surprise was perhaps because men were preoccupied and mesmerized with the sights unfolding before them or perhaps because dubbed film tracks had always portrayed such an event as a continual, even, roaring sound. The explosion was followed by a slight rumble and then all was quiet again. The silence was only broken by shocked cries of surprise.

The blast had come about one minute and 45 seconds after the initial flash. Some rough calculations were made on the spot. They showed that the bomb was just over 22 miles away, allowing plus or minus a mile or so and variation of the speed of sound.

Men left the football pitch in twos and threes but eyes were still on the giant, mushroom shaped cloud which dominated the now darkened sky. The orange glow within its dome lasted until the first signs of dawn began to lighten the horizon.

The Sun made an appearance at 7.45 am. It was unspectacular by comparison; it was second rate. It lazily inched its way above the palm trees to take its rightful place in the sky. At 8.15 am the cloud, although distorted, was still intact and aircraft were flying close to it checking levels of radioactive fallout. There was no doubt whatsoever that apart from any other encumbrance that the bomb might bestow upon us, its immediate effect had caused the adrenalin to flow through shocked veins.

The radioactive cloud had completely dissipated within three hours of the detonation. This was quite a speedy disappearance. Larger bombs than this were to follow. Even so it was this first bomb that left the greatest scar; it would remain a violent memory, in the corner of the mind forever.

CHAPTER ELEVEN

The second to the sixth.

New orders were posted. It would not be necessary to assemble on the football pitch for subsequent tests. This development was greeted with relief. At that time, it seemed unlikely that anyone would be able to relax or stay asleep during any of the preparatory countdowns, the noise of Mahatma would make sure of that, but at least the final minutes of suspense would no longer be accompanied by the discomfort of sitting on the hard and gritty surface of the pitch.

It was not long before the announcement, D Minus Two, vibrated noisily around the camp and the loudspeakers signalled that it would be two days before the second detonation.

'They're not wasting any bloody time are they?' Bill commented. 'Dust hasn't settled on the first bugger before they start the next one.'

In the early hours of Friday 27 April, the more frequent countdown commenced. Again it became impossible to maintain any real sleep once it had begun. The raucous voice of the tannoy penetrated the mind and cast aside any innermost thoughts or dreams. So even though it was still dark we got out of bed and dressed. This detonation was to be carried out just a little later than the previous one. The mess was open and it would be possible to get breakfast before the big event.

Tin trays were piled with egg, bacon, tomatoes and mushrooms. The mushrooms lay in heaps; miniature bomb shapes tumbled together at the edge of the tray.

'We'll all be sick of mushrooms with breakfast before much longer,' John muttered, moving his disgruntled gaze from the food on the plate towards the agitated loudspeaker as it blurted out yet more warnings.

By the time the disembodied tannoy-voice announced D Minus five minutes breakfast was being finished on the yachting lagoon beach. Dark goggles were put on once more. The group sat facing the direction of the pending detonation. It was still dark, the sun would not rise for another hour. In spite of having experienced the first bomb it was hard to realize that once again the night could be broken by instant light.

The final seconds were counted down. This time the flash was much brighter and heat from the bomb was intensified. It made no difference that this scene had been witnessed just two days earlier. The awesome power still produced a silently stunned and dumbfounded response from men who stood and sat, motionless, as they became bathed in the shrill light of a second false dawn.

Watches had been synchronized to tannoy times. Ten seconds were counted before goggles were taken off. A further ninety seconds was reached, then preparations made to take the onslaught of the blast. Muscles had been relaxed, slightly, in readiness but this time two explosions, instead of one, followed. It still came as a shock. The ground moved and jolted violently in quick succession. The compulsive strength of the vibration jarred every nerve. There followed a low rumble, louder than that of the previous test.

There were only a few hours of respite from tension, before the inevitable countdown began for the next detonation. This one was to be on Sunday 29 April. The distorted humped-cloud remains from the second bomb still dominated the sky. It loomed like some grotesquely changing giant, poised above the sea, indifferently biding time before claiming a human sacrifice. The huge humps moved ponderously with shimmering copper edges. They slid imperceptively and folded slowly downwards; as though holding and hoarding something secret within the shadowy valleys.

John pushed himself back. His feet were stretched out in front of him and both arms hung limply over the back of the chair.

'Next one on Sunday - church will be cancelled,' he said cynically, as he balanced the chair steadily on two of its legs.

'Births, deaths and marriages,' Bill replied. 'That's what my old Gran used to say when it came to going to church. None of us go to church anyway, except on special occasions.'

'No, but there is supposed to be respect for the Sabbath in a Christian society,' Paddy protested. 'At least that's how it's always been up until now.'

'Well it ain't any bloody more,' Bill said with a degree of working class finality. 'Before this lot's over, we'll all have the stars and bleeding stripes tattooed on our arses.'

The early hours of that Sunday morning found me sitting on a wicker armchair, alone by the edge of the lagoon. The night shift had been free from signals traffic and growing tired of the monotonous ticking of the clock in the hot, claustrophobic space of the radio cabin, I had moved outside.

The stars made up for the moonless night. They were huge. They seemed to drip, like a cascade of crystal, only to be swallowed up by the distant horizon. The silence was interrupted by the water lapping onto the edge of the sand and by the gentle rustling of the breeze. It was not difficult to spot a shooting star as it entered the earth's atmosphere and left its short silvery trail in the sky. The sparkling trail would stay for the briefest of spells before disappearing into the blackness of space. It was a pity that this place should be marred by the threatening spectacle of the hydrogen bomb.

The radio did not call me inside, so I remained there, with cigarette in one hand and mug of tea in the other. It was 4.30 in the morning.

'This is Mahatma. This is Mahatma. D minus two hours. D minus two hours.'

'Christ, Mahatma! Are you up already?' I thought, looking down from the stars to check the watch on my wrist.

The countdown continued and the announcements from the tannoy became more frequent as detonation time approached but finally, at D minus fifteen minutes, Mahatma announced a 'hold in the run'. This sequence of events was repeated four times, but each time Sunday morning persevered. It remained intact and undefiled. At 7.35 the test was cancelled until the following day.

Shortly after the last cancellation announcement I returned to the billet. Jock was sitting in bed looking surly and disgruntled.

'Mahatma is fucking up my sleep,' he announced. 'Tell you what, how about if I shinned up that pole outside and neatly snipped the bloody wires?'

He was sincere in what he was saying. With little or no encouragement he would do exactly what he was suggesting he should do.

'Jock, good idea, but there are two snags.'

'What are they then?'

'First, they would soon find out and quickly repair it. Secondly, if they caught you, you'd get hung up by your balls.'

'Aye, you're probably right,' he sighed, as though the exaggeration had acted as a deterrent. 'It was just a thought.'

Cloudy conditions caused two further cancellations. Wednesday 2 May became the appointed day for the third test. It would take place at the later hour of 9.00 am.

When the time came we stood on the beach of the lagoon and the countdown proceeded without any delays. The bomb was bigger than the previous two but not as spectacular because it took place in the broad daylight. Momentarily it appeared as though there were two unequal suns, opposite each other, in the sky. After ten seconds had elapsed and protective goggles had been removed the white-hot sphere began to dim. It hung suspended against the pale clear blue sky and began to turn red. The ball slowly began to form into the predictable mushroom-shaped cloud.

Preparations were again made for the violent onslaught of sound. This time it arrived one or two seconds earlier. It was a little closer. The blast was something that was impossible to get accustomed to, particularly because the bombs were getting bigger, or closer, each time. It was agreed that they must be warming up with the small ones first. By the end of the series the present explosion, awesome as it was, would seem like a firecracker. It seemed logical.

After the third bomb the stifling heat again saw a rapid increase in the fly population. The persistent creatures buzzed in droves around heads and trays as meals were eaten.

'Little bastard,' said John, as he swiped at one which hovered in front of his face. 'Captain Flit is long overdue. Strange the way these tests don't seem to keep the flies away.'

'Probably turn them into giant mutants,' speculated Bill with widened eyes to illustrate the horror of the idea.

'You've been reading too many science fiction comics,' John replied as he continued to slap with increasing annoyance at the insects which hovered above his food.

The idea of getting away from the more populated areas and the worst of the flies buzzing around the food was appealing. John looked out of the window and surveyed the palms swaying in the breeze. He observed that there was a whole back yard full of coconuts but nobody had even bothered to get one yet.

This was an interesting thought and we were soon walking towards the bondi between the large lagoon and the beach. Tall palms spread overhead, at one point forming a canopy which shaded out the sky. They seemed even taller now that the fruit at the top was to be reached.

It had seemed as though it would be easy enough to shin up the gangling coconut palms. The Gilbertese had always demonstrated the skill of climbing them, with confident ease. The speed and strength with which they carried out the task made it look as though very little effort was involved. However for us it proved impossibly difficult. Every time part of the trunk was scaled a point was reached where there was nowhere to gain hold. Then came an agonizing slip downwards. This explained why the Gilbertese used looped rope, across their strong and muscular backs, as an aid to climb the tree.

'There's a knack to getting up these,' Bill remarked looking at sore and scraped ankles. 'And we haven't got it.'

He slipped painfully down the nobbled trunk after a last determined effort to conquer a tree.

We turned our attention to the surrounding ground in the hope that some windfalls might be lying around. Time was spent in a thorough search but the only coconuts to be found were ones that had taken root and had begun to rot.

Feeling frustrated at the thought that something seemingly so easy was proving difficult, Bill picked up a handy sized piece of coral and aimed it towards the top of a palm which held an abundant crop of the green fruit. The coral found its mark. One of the nuts became dislodged. It swished through the palm leaves and fell to the ground accompanied by a triumphant shout from the successful marksman.

Using this method there were soon many coconuts scattered on the ground. They were picked up and piled at the base of one tree; a mound of green husks which housed hairy brown coconuts inside. Everyone congratulated themselves on being more skilled in these surroundings than they had ever been at the coconut shies of fairs back home.

The problem of transporting the haul was solved by making a stretcher out of two palm branches. The branches were placed, side by side, then the leaves were tied together to form a hammock. With the stretcher fully laden we made our way across the ankle deep waters of this part of the lagoon, to the billet.

Outside, in the shade of the verandah surrounded by a mound of coconuts we set about trying to remove the thick husks. The small penknife that was being used made little impression on the tough green fibrous casing. Some time was spent struggling with the first coconut.

A Gilbertese was sweeping the road in front of the verandah. He moved slowly and carefully. He watched the proceedings with increasing interest and continually looked away from the dusty road surface towards the pile of coconuts. Finally, he stopped his work and came over towards the inept group.

'You want I do?' he offered smilingly.

'You do a lot,' Bill said, 'And we'll give you some.'

The Gilbertese produced a small sharp knife. He made a series of cuts with the knife, but then abandoned it. He began pulling the cut sections of husk with his teeth. It was amazing the speed with which he could do this. Murmured words of encouragement were nodded at him, while he efficiently stripped away the thick casing. He was visibly pleased with the approval of his ability. On completion of the self-appointed task he pierced the soft eyes of the inner, dark-brown, hairy coconuts.

He handed them carefully to the appreciative spectators. Everyone sat drinking the surprisingly cool coconut milk for some while before he took a last swig of the liquid and again took up the job of sweeping the road.

There was much we would like to have asked him. There were unknown details about the Gilbertese evacuations. For example, how long they stayed in the ships during each test, or how far they were taken, or whether it was true they were kept below decks and shown films but the shared language proved too limited to answer such questions.

On Friday 4 May, men again congregated on the beach, at the appointed time. By now most of them were not wearing radiation badges around their necks. The piece of chord to which each badge was attached irritated as it chaffed against the skin. It was becoming common practice to keep the badges in pockets or tied to the belt loops of shorts.

The fourth test in the series was witnessed and it was hoped that there was no question of excessive radiation. There was annoyance that there had been so little information given about the dull grey warning tablets. I put my hand in my pocket and felt my radiation badge. I hoped that it would be a safe insurance. I hoped that it was primed to warn well before any effects could touch us.

The looming death cloud from the fourth bomb had begun to disperse and we walked along the beach of the lagoon. At the water's edge a large black gull was struggling in the shallow waves. It had managed to get close to the beach but scurried back deeper into the water as we approached making a vain attempt to fly away.

'Looks like he's got engine trouble.'

The unfortunate creature completed a half circle in the water and landed back on the beach. Paddy bent down to take a closer look at it.

'Looks like a damaged wing. One eye doesn't look too good either.'

'Don't pick it up, Paddy,' warned Bill. 'It may have been nearer to the bomb than us.'

'I know. I'm not daft. It could have crash-landed after the flash.'

It would be only a matter of time before the gull either became fish food in the water or starved to death on land. It would be better off in the sea; at least death would be quicker and the fish could get their revenge. Paddy picked up a piece of driftwood and pushed the bird back into the waves again. Once in the water the bulky seabird completed another half circle and instead of heading out to sea it ended up on the beach again. It looked like a clockwork toy that can only go one way round when it is wound up and let go.

'Doesn't want to leave us, does he?' Bill observed.

Further interference was withdrawn. The bird was left, as he had been found, fluttering weakly at the water's edge.

Feeling ill at ease with the idea of the wildlife caught up in man-made misfortune we walked further along the expanse of beach towards the yachting marina. Here we found Paul. He was squatting on the coral sand surrounded by folds of grey canvas. He was working on one section of it and was repairing a large rent in the middle of the sail. He completed the patch with a last few careful stitches.

'That's that,' he declared proudly.

He proceeded to neatly fold up the sail. He had a large canvas hold-all in which he stowed away the sail-needle and thread he had been using. As he put them away, a brand new harpoon gun was clearly visible among the other contents of the bag.

'You, er, managed to get a harpoon then,' Paddy said, bending down to take a closer look. 'Got anything with it yet?'

'Only that sail that I've just patched up,' Paul replied with a sheepish grin. 'The shot went a bit awry and ended up going through the sail. I'm probably not used to the gun yet.'

We asked him how the gun worked.

'Just got time to show you before I sign on for work,' he said.

He selected a cruel looking harpoon and quickly fitted it to the gun.

'There!' he said proudly. He pointed to a nearby coconut outer-husk, which was lying on the sand. 'Watch this,' he said confidently as he took up a position some way from the husk and aimed the harpoon at it.

The missile left the gun with a sharp metallic twang. We followed its course with interest but realized immediately that it had not landed where Paul had intended. For his part he stood stock still, staring in disbelief. Then he started to repeat his favourite swear word over and over again to himself. The harpoon had landed straight through the middle of his neatly repaired and folded sail. We left the beach trying to suppress our mirth. The sounds of Paul's frustration rang in our ears. We glanced back and saw him pummel the sand heavily with his fists.

The next day when I called in at the NAAFI to replenish my cigarette supply Paul was already in the shop engaged in animated discussion with the shop manager.

He was complaining about the harpoon gun that he had so unsuccessfully demonstrated. 'Through the inaccuracy of this damned thing I've got a sail on my boat that looks like a patchwork-fucking quilt.'

The manager told him amiably that the harpoon was meant to be used under water and that these things take a little getting used to.

'Getting used to?' echoed Paul. 'I tell you, there must be something wrong with it. I've had the bloody thing a fortnight and although I'm no William Tell....'

The manager interrupted to patiently point out that William Tell used a crossbow, not a harpoon.

'Well whatever,' Paul continued. 'That bloody thing fires round corners. Even the fish are taking the piss out of me.'

The manager examined the harpoon gun and noticed the green, flaking paint along the edge of it. He surmised that the gun seemed to have had a hard life in the past two weeks. Paul's face coloured slightly. I for one knew that he had thrown the gun down in a rage.

'Well, er, I dropped it, didn't I,' came the weak sounding excuse.

With a sigh, the manager pointed out that the damage to the gun would not help his case when returning it for a replacement. Finally he agreed to give Paul another gun. He left the counter and walked wearily into the rear stock room. Paul turned round to look at me.

'William Tell!' I echoed derisively and laughed. Paul shrugged confidently.

The manager returned with the replacement. He commented sulkily that this was the last of his stock until the arrival of the next delivery. Paul was satisfied with himself and gratified that he had got his own way. He wanted to try the new harpoon immediately and after leaving the shop we walked to the sand pools which lay in an area of shallow water, beyond the church.

The pools glinted in the hot sun as though a myriad of tiny mirrors lay just beneath the surface of the shining water. The edge of the lagoon lay warm and gleaming but seemingly lifeless. We could find no fish, not even a sand shark. It was as though the marine life had received prior warning that Paul was coming; that he was armed and ready for them. Undeterred he suggested that we go out on the yacht to test the new gun at the earliest opportunity.

We returned to the beach, three days later on Tuesday 8 May to view the fifth test. The sight of it still held an overpowering fascination. Some time was spent talking after the blast had occurred; eyes focused on the huge, dominating cloud. It was difficult to break the spell of fascination at the sight. It was difficult but not impossible. From now on we were to spend much less time on the beach of the lagoon.

After the fifth test the hot sun beat down throughout the day. The clouds were never very effective. They were thin and moved quickly. Constantly evaporating they rarely blocked the overhead sun and rain showers almost never lasted more than ten minutes. On this day, there was not one cloud in the bright blue sky.

As always, it was only marginally less hot as evening drew in. We sat around, lethargic and bored, smoking one cigarette after another. Jock's absence had hardly been noticed.

Just before midnight an American jeep pulled up at the end of the billets. As the door slammed shut Jock's voice was heard bidding his companions goodnight and thanking them for a pleasant evening.

'Goodnight Lootenant,' came their reply.

The sound of the departing vehicle faded into the night and some time elapsed before Jock entered the room. He was carrying two large cans of buttermilk and some food. He was dressed in civilian clothes and was looking extremely contented, which led to the query, 'What's all this loo-tenant business, then?'

'Oh, that,' he replied. 'I've been in the Yankee Officer's Club all evening. Let them think I was a British officer. That's why it was some time before I came back here; I had to start walking towards the officer's quarters, didn't I.'

'You'll get bloody done if you're found out.'

'I don't think so,' Jock answered. He was swaying slightly on his feet. 'Besides, it's not as though I was in uniform is it?'

He placed the cans of milk unsteadily, on the top of his locker. 'I've been invited back tomorrow,' he said. 'Any of you fancy coming with me?'

His invitation was unanimously declined.

'Didn't have to buy a single drink,' he carried on. 'They wouldn't let me.' He opened a can of buttermilk and lifted it up towards us. 'Fancy a wee drop?' he offered.

Again there was a consensus declining the offer.

'Lines the stomach after a good drinking session,' he knowingly informed everybody as he swilled the milk from the quart sized can. Gurgling noisily, he drained the contents of the can. He saw that everyone else was trying to get to sleep so he turned off the lights and got heavily into bed.

Less than a quarter of an hour passed before a slurred voice said, 'I don't feel so good.'

There were thumps on the floor as Jock clambered out of bed. His angle-poise lamp was aglow and it outlined his silhouette which was tottering towards the door. There was a noise which sounded like a large sack of potatoes being thrown on a bed of gravel.

Jock was lying face down on the small coral rocks outside the room. He was groaning.

'Thought you said milk lines the stomach?' I said, having followed him out without feeling the slightest tinge of pity for his demise.

'The ground is falling away,' he whispered hoarsely.

'My bit's all right. By the way you'll probably find that milk only lines the stomach before booze, not after it.'

'Have you got no sympathy man? I'm as bloated as a puffer fish,' he moaned.

126

'Not a lot of sympathy, Lootenant. I only came out to make sure you didn't hurt yourself.'

After being sick he sat on the coral for a while, starring vacantly in front of him, before returning to his bed. Then all was quiet.

It was Wednesday 9 May at 6.00 am. Surprisingly Jock woke up to the sound of the tannoy showing no signs of any ill effect from the previous night.

'What happened last night?' he asked with a look of innocence.

'You made yourself a Flight Lieutenant. You were as pissed as a newt, sick as a dog and as welcome as sand in a poof's vaseline tin. Other than that, nothing,' John replied.

'I must have had one too many.'

'One's not the word,' yawned Bill as he pulled protective goggles over his eyes.

There was a silence and then the room shook with the horrendous noise from the sixth test explosion. Every nerve jarred with its shuddering, callous, cruelty.

At 9.00 am that day the arranged meeting on the beach with Paul took place. Sails were set and the little yacht headed towards the middle of the lagoon. Although now fading the cloud from the morning's test spread upwards. It still dominated the skyline. It hung suspended as though it had been written in the sky. It was a huge graphic symbol of intimidating power. Beneath it, perhaps, a man should have felt unimportant; the kind of insignificance felt in a city of skyscrapers which vie with each other to show off power and success in a frenzied, competitive stretch towards the biggest and the highest.

As usual I pushed these ideas to one side of my mind and anyway I had begun to feel indifference, possibly even contempt, at intelligent people spending time, wealth and self-congratulatory effort on such a spectacle. It was possible to be very clever at doing stupid things.

In the boat we seemed to be at harmony with the natural surroundings. The spinnaker was up and the prow of the boat skimmed across the lagoon barely touching the surface. When far enough out the patched canvas sail was lowered and we drifted slowly in the peace of the waters, until the first large fish was sighted.

Paul was gratified to find that he had no difficulty in using his new harpoon gun but he did not do much fishing. In fact he only made enough accurate catches to confirm to himself that his previous lack of success was due to the faulty gun, not his lack of skill. I hardly touched the gun, the idea of any kind of unnecessary killing had lost its appeal.

Several relaxed and tranquil hours were spent in the boat until finally we turned towards the marina. The breeze pounded into the sails as the boat raised and bumped its way across the choppy waters, the wooden hull thudding against the ripples as it went.

Later in the billet I settled down to write home. A short while was spent engrossed in this activity. Then I paused to think; trying to reflect on suggestions for names to give the baby when it arrived. My gaze fell on the small black and white photograph of Jacky which was propped up on the locker. Looking at the picture made me wonder how she really was; whether she would have altered at all when I saw her again.

My mind drifted back to the summer's day when the photo had been taken. It was a hot afternoon and we had been swimming in the estuary creeks. Laughing, we slid down steep muddy banks, splashing heavily into the warm salty water which always stayed in the creeks as the tide moved slowly, miles out to sea. We lay happy, pillowed on the springy, warmly-scented, marsh plants, until the tide had turned. I felt I had grown too used to being away and a resentment began to engulf me.

Finally the letter was written and I fell into fitful sleep. Dreams wandered into images of a moving, steel grey, estuary sea. The sea reached up to mountains of cloud, voluminous white curtains pulled across patches of warm blue sky. Then somehow the waters changed. Suddenly, they were deathly still. They became a sparkling bright emerald expanse which stretched lifeless, for ever, with nothing else beyond. And over the strange water, motionless and quiet hung just one solitary, glittering, cloud.

CHAPTER TWELVE

The island from the seventh to the twelfth

It was early morning and the tannoy stabbed into me like a knife. It was Friday 11 May. I was tired, very tired. I remained in a semi-conscious dream-like state until the final few seconds of the countdown. Suddenly, vaguely aware that something was about to happen, I raised my head and looked around the room. Paddy and Bill were lying awake in bed. They were wearing goggles. John was a lifeless heap under a sheet.

Automatically my outstretched hand groped for the dark glasses that lay on top of the bedside locker. My fumbling fingers found them and placed them over my eyes just before 'zero'. Through closed lids, as well as the protective lenses, the brilliant flash of light was a pale orange glow in front of the eyes.

Nature has a way of demanding the fulfilment of bodily functions whatever circumstances prevail. The light began to ebb. I removed the goggles, leapt out of bed and ran, naked, to the bush outside our room. The bush, amazingly still healthy and unwithered, was known to the billet's inhabitants as the piss-bush. This was because it was used on the odd occasion, to save the laboriously long walk to the latrines. The act of relief was completed in record time. I was back in bed before the blast from the seventh bomb shook the room violently, causing tin trays to fall from lockers.

'Noisy bloody Yanks!' Bill commented. John still lay motionless in bed. 'Is he dead or something?' Bill asked.

'Sounds as though he's snoring from where I am,' came the reply.

'You're right - how the hell can anybody sleep through that lot?'

Bill walked over to John's locker. He picked up a small bottle of tablets. He shook the bottle and examined the contents carefully. Then he held them aloft and declared, 'Easy when you're using sleeping pills.'

John awoke very late. He was feeling quite pleased with himself for having 'missed a bomb'.

'More tablets tonight, John?' Bill asked him.

'Maybe, maybe,' came the dry, relaxed reply, from the Corporal.

He had been seasoned by the Suez Conflict and he seemed completely satisfied with the steps he had taken to curb any disturbing effects from the bomb on him.

On reflection it was at about this time that the real difficulties began. Mahatma's constantly aggressive presence, as well as the overwhelming threat of the bomb, was beginning to take root like a cancer. The effects were not very noticeable at first but gradually many men became increasingly depressed. Some drank more heavily and it was the Americans in particular who became more accident-prone.

The dangers increased at night. This was the time when people dropped their guard. The island then seemed to awake from its suffering and become ever more vicious. There were many horrific accidents on the dusty tarmac roads and most of the accidents happened *en route* to the American Main Camp.

There was one night when we were travelling along the road to Main Camp. It was after the sun had set. We drove in a Land Rover some distance behind an American jeep. The jeep was travelling at a comfortable speed on the correct, left-hand, side of the road. Suddenly, as if from

131

nowhere, blinding headlights appeared. They were directly facing the jeep. They were on the wrong side of the road.

The driver of the jeep reacted immediately. He did his best. In those few vital seconds the idea that he should be on his usual American side, must have crowded into his head. He swerved instinctively; to the right.

The facing lights also had one last second in which to decide what to do. The realization instantly dawned that, in this place they should not be driving on the right. Like the eyes of a wild cat springing at innocent prey they decided that there would be no escape. They also swerved but to the left. They remained facing and made impact certain; like magnets that must meet.

There was no more time. The men stood no chance. Shouts were swallowed by the scream of tyres and brakes. The vehicles careered into each other. Metal smashed and shuddered against metal in a deadly embrace. Then everything was still, except one wheel which spun quietly, on the upturned jeep. The blood that flowed did not look red in the light that glimmered from our headlamps; it stained black against the ghostly coral dust.

It was as though the island during the day contented itself with gradually rotting away equipment with its humid breath. Then at night it pounced, snatching at the twentieth century to wreak a revenge against the intruding gadgets. The Island was native and it wanted to stay that way. The death toll was mounting. At least ten Americans had now been killed during the short time that they had been on the island.

I looked at the still, lifeless bodies, tumbled in the tangled wreckage and felt that it was somehow necessary to come to an understanding with the island. It seemed right to realize that this was not the place for pride in the progress of modern man.

But, of course, progress did continue and, on the 12 May the eighth of the current series of twentieth century devices was detonated. It shook the island, whipped the sea and bathed the lonely atoll with the inevitable, powerful, and poisonous light.

At this time work at the radio broadcasting station became even more of a haven. John had his sleeping pills for soundproofing against Mahatma and I had the station as a retreat. It also had the advantage of being air-conditioned against the suffocating heat outside and best of all its main concern was music and laughter.

The comedy came in the form of BBC record transcriptions of popular programmes. These included favourite shows such as *The Goons* and *Take It From Here*. It was possible to escape, at least for a short time, into another zany and strange world. Strangely enough it was one that almost seemed to possess more sanity than events happening directly outside the four egg-boxed walls of the broadcasting station.

Playing the piano remained another escape. Both Jock and I peddled a certain brand of music wherever pianos were to be found on the island. We were still using the best piano for practice; the one to be found in the room behind the church. Unfortunately this instrument also began to feel the strain. It was when playing a particularly frantic left hand that a dull twang resounded from under its lid. This brought our musical efforts to an instant halt.

The broken string was still reverberating as Jock complained, 'It's your bloody boogie-woogie! It had to happen sooner or later. Thumping the hell out of it for so long.'

There was neither piano-tuner nor spare parts for musical instruments on the camp. Jock sat pondering for a while, mulling over the problem. He eventually decided that the answer lay in one of the two pianos which belonged in a place used by members of the RAF only.

This location was the RAFA Club. The instrument that he had in mind was tucked away in a corner of the club. It was never used because of its dilapidated condition. It was more than likely, Jock deduced, that some strings of the spare piano might still be intact. He decided to go and find out.

Later that afternoon, shortly after the RAFA bar had closed, Jock led the way into the club. He held a pair of pliers in his hand. We removed the front panel from the ruined piano and looked inside. Luck was with us; the required string was still intact.

It was more difficult than had been imagined, to turn the rusted tensioner. The activity kept us engrossed for a considerable time. At one stage in the proceedings, an inquisitive eye started to peer through the shutter over the bar, but little heed was paid to it. At last, the precious string was freed. It was wound into a coil and then taken to the room at the back of the church. The piano was restored to its former glory.

Within an hour an NCO had put in a formal request for a charge to be made. The eye peering through the shutter had belonged to him. We were now to be charged with stealing the piano string and the Section Warrant Officer was outlining the charge. He was very curious to know what had happened.

'It was due to be chucked out anyway,' Jock protested. 'We haven't stolen anything. Merely re-deployed its use to the church piano.' He then added, with studied piety, 'A more worthy use than it's ever had before.'

'Seems harmless enough to me,' commented the section Corporal who stood at Jock's side.

After the initial surprise at the threatened charge, it was decided to try to obtain support from the padre. This was in the hope that as an officer, a Squadron Leader, he might be able help in the matter. He was sought out and the situation was explained to him. When told of the

NCO's charge, he raised his bushy eyebrows and murmured an expletive under his breath. This was astounding. It sounded distinctly like a most unclerical 'stupid cunt'.

'Beg your pardon, sir?' I said.

'Oh,' the padre replied, 'The NCO concerned, has perhaps been a little over-zealous. Leave this to me. You seem to have been given some trouble after bothering to use your initiative.' He then let his own self interest slip into the conversation. 'Church piano up to scratch now, is it?' he asked. He tried not to sound too concerned.

He was assured that the church piano was, without any doubt, the best piano on the island.

'Good - I'll see what I can do for you.' He asserted positively.

There was no more discussion and we left. As soon as the door was shut, we stopped in our tracks. 'Did he swear?' we questioned each other simultaneously in astonished disbelief.

It later turned out that the padre's influence did extend to secular matters as well as religious affairs. After this, no more at all was heard about the piano string affair and the little church room continued to reverberate at regular intervals with the usual improvisations.

The day after the piano fracas had been resolved, a trip to Main Camp was being discussed. Although doing his best to intrude Mahatma was hardly noticed. It had been decided that the shopping at the American base exchange should be sampled. There were 'goodies' there that could not be got at Port Camp and the cigarettes were cheaper, although Bill was quick to point out that the American cigarettes needed to be cheaper because they 'tasted like horse-shit' anyway.

At intervals along the roadside to Main Camp, now lay several mangled and twisted piles of metal that had once been jeeps. Affixed to the wreckage were crude white-painted epitaphs, 'WARNING! DRIVE TO THE LEFT! FOUR DIED ON THIS SPOT. THREE LOST THEIR LIVES HERE. DON'T LOSE YOURS. DRIVE ON THE LEFT!!'

The paint-runs from the lettering added a sinister touch to the warning notices. It would have looked even more effective still had they been painted in red.

After purchasing the cheap cigarettes at the base exchange John called the others over to look at the rows of chewing tobacco that were on display. We were marvelling at the fact that the packets boasted many different flavours when an American Master Sergeant turned to speak to us.

' Hey, try some of this.' He had selected a packet of Bourbon flavoured chewing tobacco. 'It'll clear your throat,' he promised.

His offer was declined but he grinned showing nicotine-stained teeth.

'Like most things else, I guess. It's an acquired habit.'

He paid the cashier. He unwrapped the pack, pulled out a piece of the hard tobacco and put it into his mouth. As he chewed, he saw that we were watching him and he once again offered, 'You guys sure you don't wanna try some?'

Most of us declined with positive assurance but John did not sound as convincing as the rest. He finally succumbed to the American's mild pressure. He tugged a piece out and eyed it uncertainly.

'Jus' put it in yer mouth and chew it, son,' the American urged.

All eyes were on John as he gingerly put the plug in between his lips. After a few seconds of slow chewing, with seeming relish, he smiled, 'Bourbon, eh! Not bad!' He half shook his head to accentuate the approval.

'There you go!' said the American Sergeant, looking pleased and moving towards the exit. 'See you guys around, huh?'

Everyone was still looking at John. He nodded an energetic and reassuring farewell to the American. His mouth was closed and he was still chewing but we were feeling a little puzzled. John watched his benefactor turn out of sight. He did not say a word but as soon as the American disappeared the Corporal's face changed expression. His eyes screwed up and he looked as though he were about to vomit. He rushed for the open door at the end of the store.

We caught up with John outside the back of the store. He was wiping his mouth with a handkerchief.

'Vile shit!' he choked.

'Thought you liked it?' Bill commented.

'Had to say that, didn't I? True it isn't bad - it's bloody terrible. I'd rather chew a piece of cow dung than try that stuff again.'

'The man did say that it's an acquired habit,' I said laughing at his contorted face. 'You deserve another medal for that - but perhaps you did bite off more than you could chew!'

John grinned. Nicotine could be glimpsed on his teeth as he said, 'We'd better visit their Surf Club. I could do with a drink to get rid of the taste.'

'You'll have a Bourbon, of course?' Bill enquired.

'Bollocks!' John replied.

'OK,' said Bill. 'Even better. Bollocks-on-the-rocks for you.'

We walked to the Surf Club and the same Mahatma who frequented our own territory was singing in our ears.

On Monday 14 May we dragged ourselves towards the beach of the lagoon at 6.00 am. The group of five sat on wicker chairs at the water's edge and idly listened to the final countdown in total darkness. The detonation was at 6.20 am. This ninth explosion was a massive one. The fireball was many times larger than the sun as it appears in the sky. It filled and covered the morning blackness with stark and brilliant light and the deafening noise that followed shook us to the depth of our being.

Later that morning I felt in solitary mood. I walked past the church and across the coral sand which had been left hard packed by the receding tide. I entered the bondi and crossed the road that ran between the lagoon and the sea.

The ocean was more calm than usual. The white crashing breakers stayed way out to sea. They were far beyond the wide and gentle waves which curved and folded their way closer into shore. A Gilbertese man, with a hand-held harpoon, was busy searching the rock pools. He gave a friendly wave. I stood there for a while, watching him as the tide occasionally swirled about him and he patiently waited for the right moment to strike. This was not sport for him but a way of life and a search for food; his catch was to be taken seriously. He knew exactly what he was looking for, squid.

Suddenly he made his move. There was no audible whoop of delight as the harpoon found its quarry. He quickly drew the squid out of the water, removed it from the harpoon and placed it on a hook with several others.

He was pleased with the result of his work. With knowledge of the Gilbertese language more or less limited to 'no smoking', I just nodded approval. He showed off the catch by broadly extending both of his arms. The squid were draped over them and the long tentacle legs trailed from his hands and dipped into the water around his ankles. His warm, broad, friendly smile seemed to portray a contentment of life on the island that made us worlds apart. Behind him, along the horizon out to sea, were the grey-painted American war ships that anchored beyond the reef. He may have been contented with his island existence but the twentieth century had come to him with a vengeance.

Alone once more, thoughts were ever more frequently turning towards home. There was no chance of being there when the baby was born. The situation was far from unique but I felt cheated and disillusioned. Feelings of desperation turned to anger. I walked along the beach kicking holes in the sand. Aimlessly I followed the beach round to the Spit. Some newly-arrived American servicemen were disembarking from a tender. They were as white as the inside of a coconut; they would probably only remain on the island for one or two months before they returned home. This alone was enough to stir an annoyed envy.

Turning onto the road, towards Port Camp, one of the new arrivals approached, 'Hey! Do you speak American?'

My worn sandals and tanned legs, protruding from faded khaki shorts and my dust-flecked, bare chest added credence to his impudent question. It deserved an answer. His companion drew heavily on a cigarette.

'E tabu te moko,' I said to them with clipped, clear speech.

'What's he saying?' the puzzled American asked his companion.

'Search me,' his companion replied.

Then speaking slowly and carefully into my face he explained, 'We don't speak the lingo.'

Pointing to the petrol drums which littered the quayside, I said, 'It means put out the cigarette before you blow us all up.'

'Hey! You do speak American!' said the man enthusiastically, as he stubbed out his cigarette.

'English,' I said curtly. 'English.'

The answer sounded impatient and unfriendly but the new arrivals were not deterred. They were eager to talk about the island and it was some time before we parted company and I took a separate way along the dusty tarmac road back towards camp.

It was usually the case, as it had been on this occasion, that someone, or something, pulled me away from depression. It is times when you are alone that the mind is most vulnerable. I always allowed myself to be turned away from thinking too hard about the negative reality of the situation before it became too much a part of me.

This kind of self-protective mechanism did not seem to happen for some. One such person was an airman named Andy who was based in a neighbouring billet. He was young, slightly built, and spent most of his time alone. The first time I noticed that there was anything different about him was when I paid him a visit to see about buying a watch that he had for sale. It was obvious that even at this stage he was beginning to allow himself to worry too much about what was happening.

On being asked about the watch, Andy removed a biscuit tin from his locker and took out a small package. He carefully unwrapped an Omega chronometer from its silica gel packaging. He wanted £20 for it. It had cost him £28 less than a fortnight ago. He said that he needed the money. I turned the brand new watch over in my hand and saw that it was a good one; it would have been worth three times that price at home. I had not realized he had such a good one to sell. With great reluctance I told him that I could not really afford the watch just then. He immediately offered it at a cheaper price.

Wondering why he wanted to lose his money so readily, I had to explain that even at the cheaper price of £18 it was still too expensive for me because I needed to save money to send home. This time he accepted the explanation and returned the watch to the biscuit tin. He offered me a cigarette and we sat chatting. After a very short time noise from the tannoy burst into the room.

'This is Mahatma. This is Mahatma. There is a hold in the run. There is a hold in the run. D minus 2. D minus 2.'

Andy looked startled by the loudspeaker's intrusion. He was visibly relieved on hearing the postponement. A worried face hid behind the ghost of a smile. He stubbed out his cigarette. He immediately lit another, his hands were trembling slightly. He waved the tin in my direction but I declined a further cigarette saying that I was trying to give them up and only smoked one at a time. He started to talk about the detonations.

'It's the blast I can't stand,' he said. 'Even a paper bag banging makes me jump. Can't help it. Tried everything to get over it; put pillows over my head and cotton wool in my ears, but nothing works.'

As he talked, he sat on the bed, smoking continuously. I left him; a nervous, worried figure surrounded in cigarette smoke.

The sight of the unhappy Andy had strengthened my resolve to try to give up cigarettes. Perhaps it had also set off an instinctive reaction to put the mind to something constructive. Whatever the reason a session at Muscle Beach seemed a good idea. Bill too had decided to give up smoking and agreed that the exercise would be a good way to start off the effort.

At Muscle Beach, in the late afternoon, the Warrant Officer was already going through his workout when we arrived. Bill stopped before we reached him and observed in a hushed voice, 'Look, he's got more bandages on. He's beginning to look like a bleedin' mummy.'

Sweat was pouring down the Warrant Officer's bronzed body. He looked as though he were standing in a shower.

'He looks like I feel,' I said.

'Don't kid yourself,' Bill chided, with a critical sideways glance.

The Warrant Officer registered that he had seen us. He paused from his exercise to say, 'Can't keep away, eh?'

'Thought we'd have a tone-up, chief,' I replied, already feeling some reluctance.

'If you lads had kept it up, you'd be like a pair of Charles Atlases by now, pair of Charles Atlases.'

A ten-minute workout was more than enough in that sweltering heat. The Warrant Officer was still exercising when we decided to finish. The perspiration was mopped from our brows and we left Muscle Beach.

As we departed, Bill said quietly, 'Look at his veins sticking out like that. Looks like they're going to burst any second. Perhaps that's what the bandages are for.'

The Warrant Officer was now stretched out on the exercise bench with his feet firmly on the ground at one end while he lifted weights from the middle of his thighs to above his head with rhythmic ease.

Another two days accompanied by the tannoy's continuous chanting, were to pass until the explosion on Saturday 19 May aroused me from a deep sleep. I sat bolt upright and glanced around the room. It was filled with an eerie light that radiated from the fireball. Jock sat on his bed propped up against the wall in the far corner.

'Thought that would wake you up,' he commented.

'Didn't even hear the countdown,' I replied. 'Must have been the beer last night.'

'Aye,' Jock sighed, 'the demon drink.'

Daybreak coincided with the ebbing light from the tenth fireball. The nuclear remains looked like a normal bank of cumulus cloud except that it was the only solitary one in the sky and it was tinged with the colour of sand. There was no queue for breakfast and it was served quickly with Jock emphasizing to the catering assistant.

'What a surprise! I note there are mushrooms on the menu again today. Canned ones too, I see.'

The caterer behind the servery took no notice and made no reply.

Bill came across to the table carrying his tray. He had a camera dangling from a loop of leather attached to his wrist. He proudly showed off the new camera to everyone and said that he had been taking pictures of the bomb. He considered that he had managed to get some good ones.

He sat down and started to load a fresh film. Then he began to explain where he had bought his new camera.

'I bought it off Andy. He'd only had it a week. He paid twenty quid for it and I gave him fourteen.'

Discussion quickly disclosed that everyone knew about Andy's strange trading habits. It was discovered that he had also eventually sold the watch for £16 and that he now wanted to sell his brand new radio. The explanation he gave was that he wanted to save money. He bought the goods on hire purchase, then sold them and put the money in a Post Office Account. He knew he would have to make the HP payments. He could not save regularly otherwise.

'Can't see the logic of it,' said Bill.

'He must be bombed out,' said Jock, not realizing that he was close to the truth.

Andy was beginning to opt out of a usual way of thinking. Perhaps to him the situation with the bomb was so illogical that he easily became carried along with a tide of confusion.

Later that day the tannoy informed us, with its usual gasping monotony that there was a delay with the eleventh detonation.

'Unfavourable winds,' said the Section Officer explaining the hold up. He then went on to say that there was now talk of a further series of tests to be scheduled for November. These would be with a new American task force. Paddy looked discouraged.

'I'm not due to leave until December. Does that mean I'll be in for another lot?' he asked. It seemed impossible that another series should be started so soon.

The Officer could not confirm anything. He knew no more than that himself. Instead he changed the subject and asked whether we knew that there was to be a launch from Cape Canaveral. The USA was putting a man into space that week.

'Only one?' Paddy mused. 'Why don't they send the whole fucking lot up including Mahatma?'

'They are only one man jobs you know,' the Officer smiled. 'Not Noah's Arks.'

'Pity,' Paddy muttered. 'Bloody pity.'

It had been six days since the previous test. It was Friday 25 May. There had been minimal signals traffic during the night shift. A few seconds before the eleventh detonation was due I put on dark goggles to look out of the window of the Telecommunications Centre.

Though it was still fearsome and overwhelmingly threatening, a somewhat smaller fireball than usual appeared in the sky. Dawn had broken and there was no spectacular show of light out of darkness. It was followed by a bang that was less violent than usual.

Directly it was over I walked through the cabin door to put on the kettle and almost tripped over a body that was backing its way from beneath the outside table. It was huddled in a crouching position. The back belonged to someone I recognized as a sergeant. He looked slightly embarrassed when he saw me. Then to make things worse for him he turned to see Bill who was sauntering down the road towards the radio cabin to take up his duty.

'It's the blast from the explosion I don't like,' the Sergeant explained, looking away from the approaching Bill and back up to me.

'Me neither Sarge,' I replied, with conviction. He straightened up; a sturdy six footer with black curly hair and I wondered how much good it would do him to hide under our table. Then I added, 'Still, it was only a little one this morning, wasn't it.'

'Yeah, not as bad today,' he said with a slightly awkward grin as he walked off.

Bill gazed after him as he went, striding confidently along the beach.

'Not as bad today?' Bill argued at the space the Sergeant had left behind. 'Not as bad today?' he repeated. 'Depends which way you look at it. Not as good more likely. I reckon it wasn't worth taking any pictures of that bleedin' little one.'

It was small incidents such as this that were discussed and used to divert attention away from too much reflection and apprehension about the bomb or what might happen if things went wrong. Even so the feeling of claustrophobic imprisonment on the island was beginning to well and truly embed itself in me.

I felt more and more restricted and discontent developed as the days went by. Jacky was due to have the baby in six weeks time; a new life there while, in this place, there was continual bombardment by the sight and sound of the instrument of death. It was hard to reconcile the two ideas.

I noticed that the others were also gradually showing signs of being affected by events. Jock, for one, was finding it hard to remain passive. His drinking habits were not decreasing. At times, it only took a few pints at the NAAFI to have him threatening to disconnect every tannoy on the island. He even started to climb up to reach one or two but they remained functional. He was also known to thrash his way out of the billet door on one occasion promising that he would reach the Auster aeroplane and fly it off the island.

'You can't do that Jock,' he was told.

'Why not? If anyone asks any questions, I'll show them ma bloody licence.'

'But you're a thousand miles away from the nearest land.'

'I'll make it to South America. I've gotta route worked out don't you worry. There's enough bloody top Nazis managed to hide there, nobody found them.'

'No, but you'd stick out like a sore thumb anywhere. You're proud of your name and you'd probably insist on wearing your kilt even in the middle of the Amazon.'

It took Bill's assurance, as the Scotsman's drinking partner for the evening, to finally calm him down and give him something else to dispute.

'It s'alright,' Bill slurred reassuringly to everyone. 'He'll be all right. They probably play the bagpipes in the Andes too you know.'

Jock's hatred of the island, and of the bomb, had grown daily. His fuse grew shorter and was finally lit by the NCO whom the Highlander associated with the piano string affair. It happened one night when Jock had returned to the billet after spending an evening at the bar. This time the bout of drinking had put him in good spirits. It cut across the subdued mood of everyone else. He was in good voice and was singing away to his heart's content. A corporal entered the room from an adjacent billet.

'Put a sock in it, Jock, will you?'

Jock was put out by this failure to appreciate 'good music'.

'I can sing whenever I damn well please.'

'Not at this time of night mate. Either shut up or I'll shut you up.'

The scene was watched by everyone lying in bed with quiet amusement. The Corporal stood near to the entrance of the door. Jock narrowed his eyes and scowled.

'Now, look here, if you don't like it, just piss off.'

The Corporal paused for a moment, then moved aggressively, fist raised, towards the Scotsman. This was an unbelievable decision. He must have thought that the stripes on his sleeve brought immunity from retaliation. There was no doubt that the mistaken Corporal acted on the spur of the moment. He could not have thought out his move thoroughly. Jock turned and squared up with the speed of a highlander under attack. What happened next was inevitable.

Even with the advantage of being sober the Corporal was not quick enough. Mayhem broke out and he was hurled through the air. I leapt out of bed in a vain attempt to catch him and grazed my right leg on a locker in the process, but I could not prevent him from striking his head against the hard metal frame of the bed. He was out cold. Jock quickly came to his senses and realized what he had done. He stood looking at the body spread-eagled on the floor.

'Shouldn't have done that, Jock.' said Bill. 'You could end up in the guardhouse.'

The Corporal lay beside the bed. He was quite still.

'Is he all right?' Jock asked.

There followed a careful struggle to move the limp body into a sitting position on the bed. He began to show signs of regaining consciousness.

Things just seemed to be getting under control, when a Warrant Officer suddenly appeared at the door.

'What's going on?' he rasped. 'All this noise...'

He stopped short when he noticed the injured man propped up by Bill, on the bed. 'What's happened to him for Christ's sake?'

'He, er, slipped, sir,' Jock said, unconvincingly.

'Slipped? On what?' The Warrant Officer was gazing efficiently around the room.

'The mat, sir,' Jock answered.

Once again the Warrant Officer glanced around.

'What fucking mat?' he sounded absolutely convinced that his own powers of observation were enough. He had the answer himself.

Jock had not realized, in his alcoholic haze, that the door mat had been left outside during the cleaning of the room that day.

The Corporal was now sitting up without assistance. He was leaning forward with his head in his hands. The

Warrant Officer turned his attention onto me.

'Did you see what happened?'

'Not exactly, sir,' I began, indicating the book on my locker. 'It all happened so quickly. I was reading a book at the time.'

'What, with that racket going on?' He turned towards Bill. 'Well?'

'I was also reading, sir.'

'Well read fucking lot, aren't you?'

'Yes, sir.'

'Shut up.'

'Yes, sir.'

By now the Corporal was on his feet. He was looking somewhat bewildered by it all. The Warrant Officer (WO) asked him whether he was all right and the dazed Corporal managed to answer with some stammering reassurance. The WO let it be known that he would want to know more about the situation in the morning. He left the room with the Corporal following close behind, holding both hands against his head.

'You're bound to be on a fizzer for this one, Jock,' I said, nursing the painful graze on my shin. 'Do us a favour, will you? Don't throw your mates in my direction any more.'

'He's no mate of mine,' scowled the big Scotsman looking sheepish but undefeated.

On the following day luck was with Jock. He was fortunate enough to have the Communications Warrant Officer as adjudicator and the proceedings were dealt with in his office at the radio cabin.

'This report I have in front of me suggests that you struck a Corporal. What do you have to say about it, Jock?'

Jock was quickly interrupted before he could say anything much other than, 'Well, sir.....'

'Pissed as a fart I suppose,' said the WO. 'Fine five shillings for disorderly conduct. Don't let it happen again.'

It took some time for the leniency of the punishment to sink in. Jock knew well that striking an NCO was a serious offence. The Corporal had clearly not pushed his case hard. This could not have been the man who had made trouble over a piano string. He was soon beside himself with glee at the outcome. Everyone in the billet was caught up with enthusiasm. Inappropriately a revisit was arranged to the root cause of the whole problem; the NAAFI bar. The Corporal was there now fully recovered from concussion. The celebrations went on until well into the evening.

It was about this time that there was worse trouble elsewhere on the island. It seemed that causing as much grief as the physical presence and discomfort of the bomb, or the accidents, or the drinking, there was something else. It was almost as if there were evil vibrations which could be picked up by the mind, like litmus soaking up acid. It was as though violence from a devil-gorgon out to sea could be absorbed with casual ease and then remain, hovering, under the surface of some of the men. Occasionally the violence erupted out into the open, or spilled into the shadows of the island. There was the night when some drunks attacked a man under the cover of darkness. They battered him and raped him.

John brought the news of this incident. The announcement of it was met by a short stunned silence. Then the news was verified by someone else; the abused man was being repatriated on the next available Hastings aircraft. Jock was the first to speak. He declared that he was unconvinced that such a thing could happen. He insisted the sailors must have been drunk.

'They were,' John agreed. 'But they still did it.'

'Seems incredible. Didn't he put up any sort of fight?' Jock narrowed his eyes, 'I'd have pulled their bloody bollocks off and wrapped them around their necks if the bum bandits had tried that sort of thing on me.'

John reiterated that the man was small, outnumbered and not all that strong. Anyway he was going home.'

Bill listened quietly to what was said. His mind was always swift to find advantage. He used humour like a witch doctor shaking a charm to ward away anything that threatened to worry him. He announced that there was an answer in this to all our problems. Everyone gave him their full attention and listened seriously and intently.

'If we all report each other for rape,' he suggested. 'Perhaps we can all get a ticket for home.'

There was another stunned silence while all concerned regretted even considering there might be any answer to their problems.

Events were now rapidly deteriorating and shortly after the eleventh bomb I was to see Andy again. He was now becoming more quiet and withdrawn than ever. I had come to the room at the back of the church to play the piano because there had been an hour to kill before taking up a session as duty announcer at the radio station. The door opened slowly and Andy entered.

'Not disturbing you am I?' he asked quietly.

He sat down by the piano in an upholstered wicker chair and placed a small portable tape recorder on his knees. Knowing his strange trading habits, it was tempting to wonder whether the tape recorder was for sale. He tentatively asked me if I could do him a favour. He was quickly told that I was not buying anything. He looked down.

'No, no, nothing to sell at the moment. I just wondered if you could play a piece of music for me to record. It's only a short piece but I like it. I don't know what it's called but it's the introductory theme music for Twentieth Century Fox films.'

The request came as a surprise, the few bars of music did not seem to come into the category of a tune but it was clear that he was perfectly serious. He set the recorder in motion and the piece of music was run through twice and then I asked him how it was.

'Good!' came the nervous reply. 'But could you do the cinemascope version. You know, they add a bit on the end for cinemascope films?'

Somewhat exasperated that such detail was expected, I turned to the keyboard once more. I wondered whether a request for an impersonation of the MGM lion or J.Arthur Rank's man striking a gong would follow. However I felt in an accommodating, easy going mood, so I played through the piece of music together with the final extra bars.'

Andy was eventually satisfied and expressed his thanks. I offered him a cigarette. My abstention from the habit of smoking, like Bill's, had been very short lived. Andy thanked me in anticipation and two cigarettes were removed from the tin to offer him one.

'Er, no thanks,' he said.

'Thought you just said you wanted one?'

'I did but ....' His voice trailed off.

'But what?'

'You touched it,' he replied weakly.

It was explained that the cigarettes had to be touched to get them out of the tin. I showed him my hands were clean enough and told him I had not got the plague. His fastidious objections had begun to irritate me.

'Fingerprinted,' he stated nervously.

'Fingerprinted?' I echoed.

'Yeah, fingerprinted. Thanks all the same though.' He walked out of the door leaving me to examine the two cigarettes. He was right, the white paper had attracted a minute amount of moisture but I was left wondering as much about his edgy manner as about what he had said.

That evening Jock was sitting outside our room on the edge of the concrete path that ran under the verandah. His feet were resting on the coral pebbles and he held a mug of tea in both hands. He looked up and gave a weary greeting. He looked depressed and, finally, a little defeated.

'I've had enough of this damned place,' he explained. 'Nothing to do but drink, smoke and get bloody sunburnt. Roll on repatriation.' He paused and glowered sullenly at his feet. He ground some of the pebbles against each other with his toes before going on, 'Was playing the piano in the NAAFI bar last night and that Andy fellow came over. You'll never guess what he wanted me to play.'

'Twentieth Century Fox. Cinemascope version?' I queried.

'He's bombed out,' said Jock looking surprised. 'I told him to piss off, after the fourth time.'

Jock went on to confirm that he had also noticed Andy's reaction to cigarettes that had been touched.

'You know,' he said, 'I feel pissed off but there is always someone worse off than yourself, isn't there? What with that bloke that got raped by the matelots. Now I'm beginning wonder how long Andy will last out with this lot?'

Jock was voicing doubts that I already felt. Andy's behaviour was becoming increasingly bizarre as though to match the strange situation he was in.

Sunday 27 May. Across a stretch of rippling water, the sun's rays were already beginning to scorch the morning sky from below the horizon. Soon the harsh and harmful artificial light would give a more instant start to the day.

A quarter of an hour passed. Then there it was. The twelfth bomb. Unfailing, it turned up as expected. It was a huge one. The cruel blinding light the deafening explosion of sound and the deadly, silent, radioactive waves joined together in one massive, harmonious celebration. A celebration of evil around the isolated and tormented Pacific island.

CHAPTER THIRTEEN

A fresh, lucky face

The last week in May produced exceptionally heavy rainfall. When the rain stopped, the lagoon took on the appearance of glass. There were no ripples and the elongated reflections of palm trees on the opposite shore made an eerie scene.

The next day, temperatures rose as the sun's rays beat down mercilessly on the island. There was no breeze. Humidity was very high. Uncomfortable, perspiring bodies were engulfed in a continual suffocating heat, without any hope of relief. Then the sky clouded over. There was no rain but thunder and lightning crashed and echoed throughout the breathless afternoon. It was as though nature herself was trying to make up for the interval between the last and the next test and was interjecting with some mayhem of her own. When the sun's rays occasionally broke through the banks of cloud it felt like hot fire caressing the skin. I thought of the broadcasting station and its air-conditioning but it was closed until evening.

A heavy mood pervaded the camp. It was not just the weather. The mail had not been delivered on schedule and this always produced a bad atmosphere. There was also another reason. An American serviceman, based at Main Camp, had sent a photograph of one of the tests to a Hawaiian newspaper. All US personnel immediately had their cameras taken from them. British personnel were allowed to keep theirs on the understanding that no more pictures would be taken of the nuclear tests and all photographic equipment had to be officially registered.

Bill was annoyed by the restrictions put on his budding photographic career. He had set up brisk business in supplying his prints to an increasing number of customers although he maintained that he had only just begun to master the intricacies of his new camera.

The strained atmosphere and the anger were alleviated at Port Camp only when it was known that a film of the football cup final had just arrived on the Hastings along with the mail. It was to be shown in the cinema that night.

'Better get there early,' Bill advised. 'The place is bound to be crowded.'

Almost everybody had an interest in the cup-final and that evening the cinema was packed to capacity. I could not bring myself to join in with the mass of sweaty bodies shouting and cheering. Instead I found myself playing records in the cool air of the broadcasting station, caring little whether or not anybody else was listening.

Torrential rain pounded the camp and the football crowd at the cinema received a thorough soaking although they remained engrossed and noisy throughout the whole evening. Bill made a bedraggled return from the night out. He stood in the centre of the room with a dripping pool of water around his feet. He took some wringing wet notes from his pockets and slapped them on the table. He peeled his sodden, squelching clothes from his body. Then, ignoring the saturated clothing, he proceeded to carefully press the money with a hot iron. He swore loudly in unison with the iron every time a spurt of steam burst from underneath it. I wondered whether his team had lost or whether he was still annoyed about the camera restrictions.

Paddy looked pensively out of the window at the rain.

'What if the rain is radioactive and our badges start to buzz, or whatever it is they're supposed to do?' he mused.

'We'll all drop down dead, with our feet in the air, buzzing in agony like flies after a Captain Flit session,' answered the disgruntled Bill as he gathered up the now dry, crisp banknotes from the ironing board and placed them in his locker.

The airless humidity continued. It had been an unusually long interval since the last test and it was not until the first week of June that Mahatma woke up and, once again, announced 'D minus 2'. Bill had just walked through the billet door on his way back from work. He registered that he had heard the tannoy with an exaggerated look of horror on his face. Then he stuck his head back outside the door.

'Who pulled your chain? Get lost!' he shouted at the tannoy. He turned round again and announced that he had a message for me.

'Just taken a note down from Hawaii. Bloke you know is coming here from Hickam for a month. Someone by the name of Brian. Silly bugger volunteered to come over here. Told me to be sure to let you know he's on his way.'

This was welcome news. A fresh face would be joining the group. Everyone else was getting increasingly depressed or bad tempered. Things had got even worse since Andy had finally been declared not fit to stay on the island. He had been sent to see a psychiatrist in Honolulu. The reason given was that he could not cope although it did seem to the rest of us at the time that he had in fact found a good way of coping. He had got off the island. That at least made sense.

I looked forward to seeing Brian again, but I could not help wondering why the Welshman had decided to come to the island. I concluded that a sense of curiosity must have motivated him. He was to arrive, on the next day's Hastings and would be working in the radio cabin.

'You're putting on weight Chas. And you've got a bit of a tan at last,' boomed the Welsh voice as Brian arrived from Hawaii and we shook hands vigorously. He was introduced to the others and I pointed out that while overeating and drinking were a problem on the island, Hawaiian food had also stretched his size a bit. He grinned and patted his stomach.

'So, you're here for a month,' I said. 'You must be crazy to leave that place to come over here.'

'Thought it might be worth seeing the bomb you see. Might never get the chance again,' he said, confirming that curiosity had spurred his visit to the island.

He was told that Mahatma had been unusually quiet recently.

'How's that?' he asked, puzzled.

'Mahatma, that's the tannoy call sign. It's used when announcing the time of the pending tests.'

'Funny name,' he observed.

'Funny place,' I assured him.

The tannoy suddenly resounded, as though reminded to come back to life again.

'You're in luck, Brian. There's one tomorrow.'

The countdown continued at the usual intervals until early the next morning by which time Brian had been shown all there was to see of the camp in a grand tour of the Port Area. He was full of interest and enthusiasm to see the bomb but, after a build up of expectations, led on by Mahatma, an anti-climax came. There was a postponement. This meant that the detonation would take place at the same scheduled hour but on the following day. It would be my shift at that time so Brian could watch the bomb from the beach with the others.

On the morning of Friday 8 June, sleep had been interrupted by incoming signals and the camp bed, used for resting on night shift, was folded away. It was 6.30 am. Several rashers of bacon had been pulled from the refrig-

156

erator and were now sizzling under the grill. A sudden movement was noticeable out of the corner of my eye. It was the ginger tom cat attracted by the smell of cooking as it wafted through the air.

'What are you doing here? It's not a good time to be roaming around.' Immediately I pulled myself up, 'What's this? Talking to a cat?'

The cat's hungry look and persistent rubbing of his lithe body against my leg, made a sense of generosity prevail. I tossed him a rasher of bacon, which he ate greedily. Then he looked around for a second helping.

'Too late, old son; all gone. You'd better go back to where you belong.' The misgiving of a moment ago had been forgotten.

The countdown continued. The scrawny beast contented himself by licking my fingers all the way back to the billets. He was reluctant to leave the fingers and, when an attempt was made to toss him in the room he clung on for as long as he could. These claws were formidable talons whose effectiveness were frequently demonstrated, by the cat's keeper. He would throw the tom against the wooden side of the billet. The cat could gain immediate purchase on the wall and he would hang there for a few moments before falling back into the keeper's arms.

At last the long claws were disentangled from my hand. The cat was put into the room and the door closed on him. On the way back to the radio cabin I pulled goggles over eyes. The motionless silhouettes of Brian and the others could be seen standing at the edge of the lagoon. I continued to walk back to work, surrounded by the thirteenth evil light.

Brian turned up with Paddy to take over from the night shift. He was full of his first bomb.

'Jesus wept!' he exclaimed. 'Why didn't you tell me about the blast? It went right through me; screwed me up really terrible. It seemed so close. Why didn't you tell me?'

'What and spoil all the fun for you?'

Brian had clearly been surprised by the awesome spectacle.

'Didn't think it would be so near. The heat flash was really hot too. A real Dante's inferno, isn't it?'

Mahatma suddenly interrupted to announce the next D minus 2.

'That's quick, isn't it?' Brian asked. He did not sound as enthusiastic for the next bomb as he had been for the first.

'Not really,' Paddy replied. 'They seem to be a bit behind schedule, so perhaps they are trying to catch up. I see the kettle's got another dent in it,' he added, examining the side of the empty battered kettle. It had fallen from the table, yet again, during the blast.

Brian wanted to know if it was true that taking photographs of the tests was not allowed. We confirmed that this was so and that it had been prohibited since the American sent the photograph to the newspaper. Brian immediately knew the one in question.

'I saw it in the paper back in Hawaii,' he said. 'Good picture too.'

The mention of photographs made me seek out Bill after leaving the others. I wanted to see whether it would put him in better temper to persevere yet again with more weight training. He agreed to another session at Muscle Beach.

The heat had subsided a little when we arrived at the beach in the late afternoon. The Station Warrant Officer was already there, going through his daily routine.

'He's only got one bandage on,' Bill observed quietly, as we approached.

'How's the leg chief?' I asked.

The WO turned around and mopped the perspiration from his face.

'Thought you lads had given up,' he said. 'The leg? Oh, it's the gunge, you know, just won't clear up. Had it for a good few months now, I can tell you.' He put down the towel, 'I've just finished but do you lads want me to put you through the paces?'

'Er,' I began hesitantly. 'Er, no thanks, chief. We're only here for a quick work-out.'

The Warrant Officer mopped his brow again and slowly walked off in the direction of the Sergeant's mess.

'Cor - that would be all I need,' Bill remarked. 'I thought for a minute he was going to stay. That bloke's a phenomenon! Ten minutes is enough for me.'

'That's twice as long as I'm staying for,' I replied, heavy perspiration already dripping uncomfortably into half-closed eyes, at the same time, feeling reluctant admiration for the resilient Warrant Officer.

After the work-out I made my way to the shower block. The tepid water brought cool relief from the sweltering heat, although this good feeling only ever lasted a very short time; the temperature and the humidity would soon entice sweat from the skin's pores. It was not long before I was lazily spread out on the beach of the lagoon.

It was now 2.30 in the afternoon and the moon made a pale, almost transparent, appearance high in the heavens. Its white-marbled face looked lonely in the wide blue sky. The day-time moon was a common occurrence in this part of the world. At night the crescent moon also played strange games. In the Southern Hemisphere it lay upside down to the mind of someone from the other side of the world.

With eyes closed in the solitude my thoughts drifted far away; 12,000 miles away. Memories came of days and nights spent with Jacky. I struggled to conjure pictures up in my mind. What is it about a woman that you recall? It is always the feeling of the whole of her that is in your mind, and that is what you want. You remember that her seductive presence could easily be carried on a smile.

I wondered whether the child would be a boy or a girl? Corinne was growing up fast, totally unaware of my existence. There would also be a four month old baby on returning home. Much can happen in a year.

A sound like that of a distant bee droned in and out of the comfortable repose. The noise was growing stronger - Oh, no, not Captain Flit! I felt annoyed and too comfortable to have to rush for shelter. Then came the realization that it could not be him; it was afternoon. His activities were always confined to the mornings only. No, definitely not Captain Flit because there was more than one engine on this aeroplane. The sound grew stronger and, without opening my eyes, I continued with the speculation.

The light Auster was the only aircraft that flew over the Port Area. This one sounded as though it were coming in to land!

I sat bolt upright at the thought. This was a clear stretch of beach for a plane to land on. A Hastings passed directly above, at a height of about 50 ft, then out across the lagoon. The Hercules engines roared at a deafening pitch. The aircraft banked and then turned, for a re-run over Port Camp. The thought occurred that the pilot must be Captain Flit gone mad!

'He's got his hands on a Hastybird and he's going to flip that great, lumbering thing under the telegraph wires!'

The plane's undercarriage was down as it passed over the road, buzzed the roof of the NAAFI building and continued its flight back to the airfield at treetop height.

This sudden, unexpected, hair-raising, flying display of the Hastings remained a mystery until that evening. It was only then that the 'buzz' over Port Camp was explained by Paul. He came up to order a drink at the NAAFI bar.

'Was that you on the beach this afternoon, Chas?' he asked casually.

This was confirmed and he was asked why he wanted to know.

'Oh, I was in the Hastybird that flew over the Port Area. Thought I recognized your swimming trunks.'

'What in God's name was that all about? I thought it was coming in to land. Was it Captain Flit at the controls?'

Paul grinned and replied, 'Trial flight around the island to make sure the bugger is running all right. Was just regular crew. They are doing another one next week. You can come if you like. Fancy a trip?'

'Er, no thanks, Paul. I saw how it was performing from the ground. Thanks all the same.'

'Was a bit hairy, wasn't it?' He grinned hugely at the thought then added, 'Even if you don't like flying, why don't you join a group of us going down to the ski-lagoon on Sunday?'

I agreed that this would be much more to my taste than dive-bombing Port Camp 'like a blue-arsed fly'!

The next morning, Saturday 9 June, Mahatma was announcing ten minutes to the next detonation.

'Nearly there, then,' observed Brian, as the little group breakfasted on the beach of the lagoon. 'Do you always come out here?' he asked.

He was told that at first we had always come down to the edge of the lagoon to see the detonations, but did not do so as frequently now. It was probably only the fact that he wanted to see the tests, that had brought us to the beach. It was added that nearly everybody had now slept through at least one of the bombs. He found the fact that anyone could sleep through it all hard to believe.

'This *is* number fourteen, Brian. The only reason we sometimes get up is through Mahatma balling about all over the camp. The novelty has worn a bit thin now.'

'You amaze me,' he said. 'But, somehow I suppose you're right. It seems strange though don't you think? I mean, you'll probably never get another chance to witness all this again will you?'

'Who knows?' I replied, staring across the lagoon at the first strain of daylight. 'Who knows. There may be such a thing as World War 3.'

The countdown continued.

'They'll never use them, though, will they?' Brian said, in a manner that seemed to ask for reassurance.

'Won't they?' I heard myself reply and I thought of Nagasaki and Hiroshima. Then I looked at him and laughed; the unacceptable thought tossed away with a smile.

'Why don't you sit back and enjoy your bomb?'

We flipped the goggles over our eyes and night was, once more, turned into day.

Only a short time elapsed after the morning's test before Mahatma was again chanting. This time heralding the approach of the fifteenth bomb.

'My nerves are shattered!'

These words were always a signal from Jock that he was feeling depressed. He was sitting at a table in the billet draining a can of Red Barrel. He finished off the beer, then held the empty can up in front of him and studied its label morosely.

His despondency had been caused by a visit to the administration office. He went there to find out whether he could to get away from the island a few weeks early. He was desperate to get some flying hours in; enough to renew his pilot's licence. He had been told that everything depended on when his replacement arrived. He had chosen to interpret this pessimistically. He was now stewing in his misery.

Brian was talking about his posting at Hickam. This did not help the situation. It was interesting but it did little to cheer anybody up; Brian's situation held such glittering prospects compared with the sparse and disadvantaged opportunities that our island presented.

He said that RAF personnel in Hawaii had extra pay. This compensated for the high cost of living on the American island. It was also easy to get an extra job there. He worked as a part-time waiter. He had managed to save a lot of money. He had friends who had formed a successful pop group. They earned an unbelievable $100 each a week. These musicians were worried. They had already stayed two years. This meant that they would be allowed to remain, in Hawaii, only a further six months, before being repatriated.

'My heart bleeds for them,' said Jock without sincerity.

'Mine too,' said Brian. 'But you can't blame them for wanting to stay on - not over there anyway.'

Brian went on to describe other perks that were his lot. American amenities could be used and RAF personnel were issued with a special uniform, made from best quality gaberdine.

'They're better than the Yanks' uniforms, man,' he asserted.

The list of advantages seemed endless and all this was on top of another image in our minds. This was the folklore fantasy that came with the name of the place. It was one of dusky, bare-breasted nubile women gyrating sensuously to the sound of whining Hawaiian guitars. Their smooth, flower-decked, brown bodies, and their primitive, grass skirts swaying to a seductive and tempting song. They would stop their dancing to offer tasty morsels from feasts of fruit with a whispered *aloha* from full smiling lips. Then they would bring fish and pork wrapped steaming, in palm leaves. Relaxed, they would lie, with dark languid eyes inviting, at a man's feet. It was true, we would have felt sadly disadvantaged and deprived, even without the nuclear bomb hovering over our lives.

The Welshman had been given the chance to stay at Hickam for another year. He was considering whether or not he wanted to take up the offer. There was considerable surprise expressed by the others that he had not yet made up his mind. Brian went on to explain that he did not want to be away from his girlfriend any longer than necessary.

'You'll probably end up rich and lose your girlfriend,' Paddy suggested, half-hopefully.

'Oh, I don't think so,' he sounded sure of himself. 'We are engaged, proper like, ring and all.'

Brian's charmed life was unassailable.

The pessimistic mood and the pervading despair, of all but one of our number, were suddenly interrupted by Paddy who dashed for the door shouting, 'Windows!'

Everybody rushed around the room and managed to close the louvre windows just before Captain Flit passed overhead.

'You blokes must be going deaf,' Paddy complained. 'Didn't you hear the fucker approach. You nearly had us drowned in fly poison.'

Dragged from his gloom the well-spoken highlander decided to draw attention to Paddy's Northern Irish accent.

'Auster,' Jock said dryly.

'What's that?' Paddy questioned.

Jock gave an exaggerated sigh, raised his eyes in the air and said, 'It's an Auster aircraft, not a Fokker.'

The next day, Sunday 10 June, we stood at the servery of the airmen's mess waiting for a fresh tray of bacon to be brought out. The countdown continued. Mahatma was informing that there was thirty minutes before detonation. Brian became edgy as the minutes ticked by. He was worried that we were 'cutting it a bit fine'

'Don't worry,' I told him. 'They don't stop serving for another ten minutes or so.'

'I mean the bloody bomb, man, not the food,' he sounded slightly exasperated.

He was told that he could hardly miss anything with the countdown surrounding us every minute as it did.

We settled down on the beach of the lagoon as the countdown continued.

'Told you there was plenty of time,' I said, looking at Brian.

'Life's a bit wild, here, isn't it?' he replied. 'In Hickam everything seems sort of orderly. Mind you, there's only a handful of us there.'

'And your very smart uniforms probably do help you retain your very high standards,' suggested Jock not looking in the least impressed. Then he added, 'You must remember that we shouldn't be here at all. Not if you think about it.'

'Bombs away!' Jock mumbled as the tannoy announced the release of the fifteenth bomb. The countdown continued until the familiar new, malevolent sun was born again in the heavens.

'Big bastard!' Paddy sighed aloud.

Brian had placed his hands over his ears but the blast that followed was unexpectedly mild for the size of the bomb. It had a surprising effect which differed from what we had come to expect.

'Made my ears pop!' Brian exclaimed.

Everyone felt the same sensation and we sat there swallowing repeatedly and blowing noses to release the pressure, while the nuclear cloud grew gradually to fill a monstrous place in the sky.

On the way back to the billets, the bomb was quickly cast from the mind like flicking a spider from an arm.

'Big treat today, lads,' I said. 'Paul's taking a wheelie down to the skiing lagoon this afternoon and then we'll wangle an evening meal at enemy camp.'

'Enemy camp?' Brian queried.

'Main Camp, where the Yanks live,' Paddy replied. 'We're not supposed to eat there unless we're on duty over there but they don't know.'

Brian informed us that he had never tried water skiing before. We told him that it was easy and that Paddy and I had only done it twice ourselves. The persuasion worked on Jock as well.

'I think I'll have a wee crack at it myself,' the Scotsman said.

'It'll be a new experience for me.'

We met Paul at the motor pool at midday and seven of us climbed into the open-top Land Rover which had been acquired for the occasion. Paul always looked the pleasure-seeking playboy and sports lover, but today his exuberance was even more marked than ever. He had a permanent happy grin on his face. We asked what it was that he was so pleased about.

'Only six weeks to do, matey. Six bloody weeks then it's bye, bye Christmas-bloody-Island.'

'Lucky sod!' came the sole comment from amongst the passengers. He started the engine and then began to sing an unrecognizable tune to himself as he drove happily along the bumpy road.

The water at the skiing lagoon was quite choppy. This made the skis bump up and down considerably more than usual. Paddy managed to complete two circuits with great difficulty and fell off just before returning to the jetty. It was then Jock's turn.

Paul was in the driver's seat of the boat. Jock was supported in the water until he was ready.

'Hit it!' he called out confidently.

The bow of the boat rose out of the water and took the slack from the rope. Jock came up to the surface. He was surrounded by gushing spouts of spray, like Neptune rising from the deep.

'Keep your arms straight,' I called after him.

The answering 'aye' turned to 'argghh!' after a few yards as Jock sank like the *Titanic*, with somewhat less grace than he had emerged from the waters.

The boat kept going, speeding through the water and Jock hung, stubbornly, to the stick at the end of the tow rope. Once again, he rose from the lagoon like a small whale hooked on the end of a line. Miraculously the skis remained on his feet but his buttocks stayed in the water for fifty yards or more. The wake caused by this stunt was sensational and it matched that of the speedboat. We stared with some fascination at this feat until finally Jock sank beneath the waves.

'Fuckin' hell!' Brian sighed, his face consumed by one huge grin as Jock's spluttering head reappeared above the water.

After three more falls, Jock managed to complete the circuit.

'What a bloody state to get into,' he said wearily as he staggered onto dry land. 'I feel as though I've had more than one enema with all that water shoved up my arse.'

Brian did not fare much better when his turn came. His efforts however were not as sensational as Jock's. By the end of the afternoon, they were both skiing very well and were almost on a par with Paddy and myself. There was no need for towels; the heat from the late afternoon sun quickly dried our bodies leaving our skin covered with the whitish powder drawn out from the salt deposits in the water.

Later tired and hungry we arrived at the American airmen's mess. Paul parked the Land Rover and we joined the fast-moving queue. The group looked totally dishevelled compared with the surrounding men in their smartly pressed uniforms.

'Aircraft maintenance crew,' Paul mumbled at the Master Sergeant, standing beside the entrance and we walked boldly in.

'Are you guys, er...'

'Royal Air Force, old chap,' Jock cut in with his best effort of a wartime pilot's accent as he walked past.

'Oh,' came the reply. 'I, er, would never have guessed.'

He was serious. When we came to examine his statement, we found there was not one piece of RAF insignia between us and, to his amazement, Brian fitted in with the group perfectly.

A day passed before a morning arrived when the air was cooler than usual. We sat on the edge of the lagoon on Tuesday 12 June with shirts on and shirt-sleeves down. The previous day, the temperature had dropped to 78°F and we had been shivering despite the presence of the sun and despite the fact that this would have been considered a hot day back home in England. It was the coolest day so far on the island.

The sixteenth bomb made its appearance on time, adding a little extra warmth to our cool bodies. The heat flash was short lived but the hated blast that followed seemed to jolt through my body. As the mushroom cloud took shape I felt strongly repulsed and thought, 'You are ugly. You are the ugliest thing that I have ever seen.'

It no longer held any fascinating appeal whatsoever. It was stark. It was vicious and totally destructive. It was an evil answer to evil.

I returned to the billet ahead of the others. A feeling of gloom had spread over me and I was unused to its intensity. Paddy was the first to come through the door.

'You look pissed off, Chas.'

'I am,' I almost resented his remark and felt annoyed that he should have detected my depression.

He immediately dispersed the antagonism by saying, 'Me too.'

Jock entered the room.

'Ma nerves are shattered,' he growled.

Brian noted the gloom and took steps to alleviate the situation.

'Just look at that,' he said, extending his arm with a freshly laundered shirt in his hand. 'Bloody laundry had put too much starch in it. You could break the bloody sleeve off.'

It was pointed out that there was probably someone working in the army laundry who had a sense of humour.

'What's your lot like?' demanded Brian.

I undid my bundle of laundry and stared at the hard bundles of cloth in disbelief.

'Same,' I said. 'I daren't unfold it.'

'Well there's nothing else we can do. We'll have to take them back,' Brian declared. 'Come on, let's give the laundry a bollocking.'

The laundry was set amongst the army billets on the other side of the football pitch. It was easily identifiable by the haze of steam rising from its midst. Outside, there were bins overflowing with empty soap powder boxes as well as a preponderance of used starch cartons.

We approached the building. An army corporal leaned against the frame of the open door, smoking a cigarette. He glanced in our direction and stood up as we approached. The conversation opened aggressively, 'Right! Who's the fucking comedian then?'

He seemed taken aback by this question. His eyes scanned his two protagonists, looking for signs of rank. There were none. We were wearing only our khaki shorts. We had always considered senior aircraftsmen to be the equivalent of an army corporal anyway. We stood there expectantly.

'What's the problem, er.....' he paused for a short time as though expecting me to identify myself by rank.

Brian took the initiative and with arms stretched out holding his shirts said, 'The bloke who done these wants screwing. Feel them. They're like bullet proof bleedin' vests.'

The Corporal gingerly reached out with his hand and touched the cuff of a shirt sleeve.

'Careful!' Brian warned, sounding concerned, 'I don't want the bloody thing broken off.'

The Corporal reddened slightly. He looked over his shoulder through the open door. A private soldier was busy inside bundling together various items of khaki clothing. Opposite him another private was attending to the washing machine. The heat in the wash-room was overpowering but they wore shirts. These were saturated with sweat.

The Corporal held one of Brian's shirts with some reverence and called out, 'Did you put too much starch in this lot? They're stiff as bleedin' boards.'

The soldier attending to the bundles managed to stifle a snigger whilst the other at the washing machine replied with an innocent look, 'No, Corp - always use it very sparingly.'

Another snigger, disguised with a cough, echoed in the room. The Corporal glanced at us and then back again at the soldier and said, 'Well, some silly sod did.'

Carefully, the Corporal took the bundles from us. He handed them to the private and said, 'Here, put these into soak for a few hours. Treat them like unexploded bombs - carefully. Got it?'

The soldier looked at us with his teeth clenched in an effort to control his mirth. He took the bundles into his arms and muttered, 'Yes, Corp,' before scurrying back inside.

The Corporal looked at us, warily, and began, 'They'll be ready for you tomorr...'

I cut him short, 'There's no hurry. As long as they are ready by this afternoon.' Then I looked at Brian, 'Come along, man,' I said briskly as though he were under my command.

This gave the Corporal cause to call after us, 'Four o'clock.'

At a safe distance, we broke into uncontrolled laughter.

'There's only one thing,' Brian said. 'He might just see us in the NAAFI or the airmen's mess.'

'Well, our officer eats there sometimes, doesn't he?'

'True. I bet that pongo Corporal is a bossy bastard.'

'Maybe,' I replied. 'But he doesn't know whether he's punched, bored or countersunk now.'

We need not have been concerned. The constant stream of irate servicemen heading for the laundry told us that we did not have to worry. The Corporal would have enough trouble on his hands to remember who was who.

Mahatma sang out at 6.15 in the morning, on Friday 15 June, the alarm that it was one hour before the detonation of the seventeenth bomb. The diffused light from the lamp outside the room dimly lit the partially inanimate postures of men stirring in their sleep. It was another half an hour before anyone made a move to get out of bed. When they did they got dressed almost mechanically. The silence was only broken when Bill drained a can of beer that had been opened the previous night.

'Jesus wept! How could you?' choked John as he screwed up his face.

'Thirsty, ain't I,' Bill replied sleepily.

'Stuck my fag-end in that last night. Thought you'd finished with it,' Paddy said with a yawn.

We went down to the beach with Brian. The bomb was not one of the largest. It almost pretended a humility which belied its lethal deadliness. The detonation was followed by a slight rumble. The light began to ebb and a small scraping sound was heard close by. It came from under an upturned boat. Suddenly the boat lifted and the Sergeant who had been under the table at the radio cabin emerged from beneath the wooden hull. He acknowledged the chanted 'good morning' with a nod. He then made his way from the beach. The group stared after him. Then Bill lifted the boat to see if anyone else was underneath.

He justified the action, 'Well, it's a two man boat ain't it? I wanted to see what was going on.'

Later on in the day three more Americans were killed in another road accident. Their total fatality list now numbered twenty. The road to Main Camp was becoming like a scrap heap; laden with wrecked jeeps and crude epitaphs. Soon, however, Mahatma was announcing the next 'D minus 2'. Bill was agitated; he looked sullen and miserable.

'How many more of these buggers have we got to go?' he asked angrily.

John reminded him that we had seen seventeen tests and that there were seven more to go. Bill did not answer. He was leaning over a letter which was spread out on his bed. He had already read it several times but he continued to look at it. He sat there, dejected, not bothering to push back the hair that hung over his eyes.

'What's up then?' John asked him.

'Had a letter from my girlfriend. She's going out with another bloke.'

He did not look up as he replied and refused to say any more for some time. It was Paddy who finally got a response from him. He did this by breezily asking everyone in the room whether they had heard the lines from a song: 'She said she'd wait till hell froze over. Sure must have been a cold winter!' Paddy whined the words, with a hill-billy accent, and then grinned around at everybody. He looked as though he were expecting the usual lighthearted response from Bill but the unhappy young man continued to look down and just retorted sourly, 'It's bleedin' summer.'

Paddy and John left the room without further comment and Bill remained looking at his letter for some time.

It was some hours, together with persuasion from Brian, before Bill decided that pining was not his style. He would take positive steps to stem the tide of self pity in which he had been drowning since reading his girl friend's letter. He had come to the conclusion that there would be others to admire a well-tanned, well-built, body when he got home. He decided that three of us would pay another visit to Muscle Beach.

It was more than surprising to find Jock already there. He looked fresh and fit. He had a strong physique and was managing quite hefty weights.

'I've been popping over here during my mornings off,' he explained as he puffed and gasped for breath on bringing the bar to rest above his chest.

'You know,' he went on. 'It helps me to stave off my craving for the female sex.'

He lifted the weights, above his head. He did this with an ease that belied their true weight.

'God knows,' he continued. 'It's been so long that I even find myself fancying the bloody coconuts! Have you seen them? They are always hanging in pairs from the palm trees?'

He stopped moving the weights and held them above his head while he looked across to the trees and then back at us.

'They hang there, tormenting, like bloody great big pairs of tits!'

We looked across and up at the tantalizing fruits. It was true enough. Voluptuous curves abounded. They hung shining, smooth and suggestive, in the hot sun.

Two days passed. We walked down to the beach of the lagoon on Sunday 17 June to see the eighteenth test. Most of the men had their own particular watching spot throughout the Port Area. They would stand about singly, or in groups of room mates. Out of the darkness, the flash from the detonation would suddenly illuminate them as though they were in total daylight.

Today was different. There was hardly anyone to be seen. The area was almost deserted. Half of our usual group had also stayed behind, in bed, their heads covered with pillows to block out the light and noise. Only Jock, Brian and myself stood breakfasting there as usual.

A lone bird was caught in the light of the bomb. It winged its uncertain, confused way against the sky. It quivered in flight when the blast finally overtook it. We stood transfixed, watching the unfortunate creature. We had witnessed this scene many times before but somehow, in the absence of men, there was nothing else on which to focus our attention other than the familiar cloud of death.

'Keep up, you bugger!' Jock murmured to the bird, as it went into a dive reminiscent of a World War 2 Spitfire.

The bird aimlessly soared and dived as though riding on an invisible helter-skelter. It tried again and again to get back control of its flight until finally it disappeared out of sight beyond a line of palm trees still lit by the power of the nuclear cloud.

Weary faces adorned Port Camp. Complaining discontent manifested itself everywhere. There was talk of general repatriation after the current series of tests but there was no foundation for such rumours. Certainly, at the communications centre we had heard nothing to substantiate these ideas.

It was fortunate that Brian was relatively fresh to the island. He did not seem to be weighed down with the same air of hopelessness or degree of despondency that was beginning to reveal itself in the rest of my companions.

He was soon to return to Hawaii and he wanted to spend an afternoon fishing, native style, with hand-held harpoon. We walked along the soft, wet coral sand, leaving a trail of deep footprints which curved, in a weaving chain, behind us. He was fascinated by the stranded puffer fish as they rocked, bloated with alarm, in the pools.

'Nothing personal,' he said, as he prodded a puffer fish and made it shrink with a loud 'plop'. 'But I'll be glad to get back to Hickam.'

He was reminded that he had only witnessed six tests, so far.

'That'll do for me,' he answered. 'The novelty is wearing a bit thin. I just want to get away from them now.'

He stopped to look at a small sand-shark quivering in the sand

'I've decided to opt to stay at Hickam for an extra year,' he informed me.

'Nice to like a place that much,' I replied. 'Don't you yearn for Wales?'

He thought for a while and explained that he loved Wales. His decision was influenced by the thought that once his service life was over he would settle down and never want to leave there again.

'Funny, isn't it?' I admitted, rolling over a small rock at the bottom of a pool to release a burst of tiny transparent fish.

'Halfway round the world and I've never set foot in Wales. What's it like there?'

'Beautiful man; I love the mountains and the lush green valleys. It rains a lot, mind, but I suppose I'm used to that. What's your place like?'

I described my home town and told him about my family. He stopped searching the water's edge and looked out to sea and asked when the new baby was due.

'Early next month. I may receive a telegram, via you, from Hickam.'

'What's it like - being a father?'

'Someday, I'm going to find that out.' I answered as I tried to remember the petal feel of a baby's skin.

That evening it appeared that still more servicemen were drinking to excess in the NAAFI bar. Cigarette smoke draped hazily about the room and seemed to find difficulty in escaping through the open louvre windows. Drunken chatter and the sound of beer cans being pierced added to the intemperate atmosphere.

'There's certainly enough piss artists here tonight,' Brian observed.

'They're all getting bombed out,' Jock slurred. 'Bloody bombed out.'

'You've got eyes like piss-holes in the snow, too, Jock,' Brian told him.

'Aye, maybe - but they're entitled to be so, after this lot. Look at poor ... what's his name...Andy. Sent home, off his rocker. Then the chappie raped by the matelots. And what about the poor sods of Americans who can't get it into their heads to drive on the left? That's just counting the ones we know about - I bet they'll be a few more candidates for the funny farm before this lot's over.'

A drunken voice called out, 'Give us a tune on the piano, Jock.'

'Aye, why not.' He got up awkwardly, looked across and asked whether I'd like to attempt a duet.

I glanced at the battered instrument in the corner of the bar and said, 'No, not this evening. Anyway that piano's fucked.'

Jock thought for a moment and nodded his head as he replied, 'So am I. So am I. We'll make a fine pair. The piano will match me perfectly.'

It was to the discordant sounds of 'Donald Where's Your Trewsers' that Brian and I left to sign on for the night shift.

On Tuesday 19 June, Paul joined our small group on the beach for one of Brian's last bombs.

'So this is where you lot hang out?'

'Pull up a conch and sit down,' I answered.

We sat there, in the dim light of the outside electric lamps and chattered idly as the tannoy crackled and chanted its message.

The nineteenth bomb was detonated and the nuclear light brought warmth to our bodies which had been chilled by an early morning breeze. In the false dawn the clear blue sky seemed to extend forever.

'Nice day,' Paul remarked, with no emotion in his voice.

The fireball expanded until the nuclear cloud began to form. Its light gradually ebbed, then held its density, to take on the appearance of a vermilion sunset. Brian gazed at the colour unfolding before us.

'Perhaps the last morning of the world will look just like this,' he said and then the crack of the blast, the sound of the devil's whip, drowned his words.

There was to be a change in Brian by the time he left the island. The change was hardly noticeable but it was nevertheless there.

'See you in Hawaii, when you take your leave there,' he said as we shook hands. Then he climbed the steps of the bus for the journey to the airfield. He still had the air of optimism about him; it seemed nothing could dent that. He still looked as though he had the ability to act as a magnet to good luck, with every step that he took. Perhaps now, though, there was a slight difference.

It was as though now he understood that a question mark always hangs, perpetually suspended, against all good fortune.

CHAPTER FOURTEEN

Bighorn, Starfish Prime and the last bombs

Bill entered the radio cabin to take over his shift. He brought with him the news that the largest bomb yet was to be included in the last of the detonations.

'It's going to be a whopper. Mahatma'll even call it by its special name - Bighorn,' he informed.

'Sounds obscene, as well as a bit General Custerish, doesn't it?'

'As in Battle of Little Bighorn, Chas?'

'Yeah, and that turned out to be a disaster for the Yanks didn't it? Let's hope they've got a few Indians on their side this time.'

On returning to the billet, I tried to write the usual daily letter home to Jacky, but found it very hard to concentrate. What was there to write, apart from megatonnage and countdowns? The letter writing was postponed. Laying on top of the bed, my thoughts drifted back to first encounters with bombs - albeit those of the conventional type.

At the age of five, living in London, during World War 2, the most important thing about bombs was not the death and destruction that they brought. To a child's mind, their main purpose was for you to be able to collect pieces of shrapnel to compare with that collected by friends.

Barrage balloons were always suspended in the sky; so much so that it seemed they had a right to be there, just like the clouds. We had never known the sky otherwise. Most nights the heavens were blotched with an orange glow and criss-crossed with the white beams of search lights. All this had seemed a natural way of life. At that age the anxiety of adults rarely affected us.

After the siren had sounded a visit to an air-raid shelter was more like a game, especially if a friend was staying at the time. The distinctive sound of an enemy V1 would fill the air and then silence. The rocket's engines had cut out. We knew how long the rocket took to land and we started to count, to find out if we would be the ones to die. When safety was certain we waited for the sound of the explosion to arrive. There would be a shattering blast somewhere in the distance. The devastation was somewhere else.

It seemed hard to imagine the outcome and the greater carnage of that war if atomic weapons had been attached to those rockets. These, and similar thoughts, remained throughout the rest of the morning.

There was now an atmosphere of complete lethargy and total exhaustion about the camp. There was a fatigue which could not be wholly explained by a greater consumption of alcohol or by the fact that the tannoy broke sleep patterns as frequently as it did. Mahatma alone showed no signs of growing tired as he shouted out 'D minus 2' for the twentieth detonation.

'You're no longer funny, Mahatma,' yawned Paddy as he finally woke up and sat on the edge of his bed, his shoulders rounded and his eyes half closed.

'You're back in the land of the living then?' Jock asked mockingly.

'You call this living?' Paddy responded, with a low, tired voice.

'You look shagged out,' Jock told him. 'Don't tell me you slept through that lot going on out there.'

'Must have,' Paddy replied sleepily. 'As it is I'm forcing myself to sit on the edge of the bed. Still bloody tired.'

He had remained in exactly the same position with his hands gripping the side of the bed but now, as though to illustrate what he was saying, he slowly let himself fall back until he was again lying prone on top of the bed.

The air of quiet indolence remained in the billet although it was now well past nine in the morning. There was very little movement and no effort was made to think or talk.

Paddy finally grew impatient of the lethargy; he refused to succumb completely to the present wave of despondency. It was probably an inbred Protestant ethic that demanded he put up a fight against it and he set about organizing himself with determination. He arranged that we would go to the shop when it opened at ten o'clock. Racquets and balls would be hired with a view to playing a first game of tennis since arriving on the island. It was easy to go along with the idea in the hope that some kind of action might help to dispel the feeling of fatigue.

On arrival at the tennis court a coin was promptly tossed in the air to determine first choice of end and service. The sun beat down mercilessly. The air was chokingly hot with the ever present coral dust particles constantly carried in the air by movements of the breeze. It took only one service to convince Paddy that he needed his sunglasses. He fumbled in his pocket for them and put them on. When he came to serve his next service, the glasses bounced from his face onto the hard dusty court. He picked them up and carefully bent the sides to make a tighter fit. He was beginning to feel edgy.

After a few minutes, it was time to change ends and face the sun.

'Might have brought your own glasses,' Paddy complained, when he reached the net. He removed the sunglasses and handed them over stoically.

The glare from the off-white coral made it almost impossible to see the oncoming ball, even with the glasses on. Soon the sunglasses were steamed up. Sweat was running down my forehead into pained eyes and blinding them. An improvised headband made out of twisted handkerchief lasted only a very short time before it had to be wrung out.

Frustration gave way to temper. The trade wind whipped up more layers of coral sand, which stuck to clammy bodies to form crusty patches on legs and chests. Swearing complaints filled the air.

'Sod this for a game! Poxy sand's even getting under my foreskin!'

Foul language continued to fly alongside the tennis balls. With tempers becoming completely frayed. Suddenly someone appeared standing by the court entrance. It was the tall calm figure of the RAF chaplain.

'What's this, then?' he enquired with a smile. 'Judging by the language I'd say it sounds like England against Ireland.'

'Not exactly, sir. It's more like England and Ireland versus the elements.'

'Ah, I see. Wrong time chaps.'

'Wrong time, sir?'

'After four,' the padre stated. 'After four the sun is in a more westerly position and a little cooler.' With that piece of advice he bade us good-day and strode off towards the church.

'Got fed up with it any-bloomin'-way,' Paddy mumbled, as he headed towards the shower block after returning the racquets. It was intriguing how in the face of island's many frustrations the young Irishman did not allow himself a more indolent life.

Lying in bed in a dream-like state, sporadic announcements from the tannoy stabbed into the brain. It was difficult to remember recent thoughts. Then recollection came. Friday 22 June, there had been questions in my mind about the bombs that the USSR had tested much closer to home and the dense populations of Europe. How much care had the Russians taken with wind direction and atmospheric conditions? Had they made any mistakes or done any damage through ignorance? If there had been any errors would we ever know? It became difficult to make my body wake and respond; there was only exhaustion and the desire to sleep. Finally I drifted back into unconsciousness and no more was heard of the countdown of the twentieth bomb.

'This is Mahatma. This is Mahatma. D minus one to Bighorn. D minus one to Bighorn.'

Within a matter of hours, Bighorn was called off. It was postponed for at least a day. The constant lethargy remained and by Sunday exhaustion completely engulfed me. I felt as heavy as lead and was too tired to get out of bed. There was no logical reason why this should be; sleep had been normal throughout the previous night.

Lying in a stupor there was one idea uppermost in my mind. It was the idea that it should be easy to live with this situation. Like many of the other men on Christmas Island I had a father who had fought in war, and grandfathers who had battled in World War 1 trenches. They would have lived beside constant bombardment in the knowledge that it was aimed at them. It *should* not be difficult to cope with these tests. I thought of the mustard gas in the 'Great War' and of its instant torture and its cruel, crippling effect. Now it was the nuclear bomb with a poison that could not be smelt, seen or heard, but with effects that could keep up their torment beyond a lifetime and into new generations yet unborn.

Eventually, the tiredness completely engulfed me and sleep came. In brief spells of dreams thoughts came of lying, softly cushioned away from the world, not feeling too hot or too cold and veiled from anything the mind did not want to see. Then the dreams slipped away and drowned once more back in a black subconscious sea.

During Sunday, the idea of getting up, in brief periods of wakefulness was quickly abandoned in the face of the negative response from an unwilling body. There was no fever, or illness, just an almost drug-induced state of sleep.

Various comments were made by people during the course of the day but these, whatever they were, went unanswered. Even the tannoy outside the window failed to penetrate the semi-conscious stupor or state of sleep, until late in the evening. Then, yawning hugely, I managed to raise myself up and sit on the edge of the bed, dazed, leaning on both hands for support.

I remained in that position for some time, until Paddy said, 'You were sleeping like the bloody dead. You okay now?'

It was too early for words to form but something, that resembled a 'yes', passed automatically through tired lips.

I then discovered that everyone suffered bouts of exhaustion at various times throughout the tests. They put it down to a possible build up of nervous tension. Perhaps in some way the body will opt out for a while. In an almost trance-like state, I dressed slowly and wandered to the beach of the lagoon. The cool, reviving trade winds gradually brought me back to a more normal condition. I felt a little more awake by the time the yacht club was reached.

There was a sound, like that of a guitar, drifting tunefully in the wind. At first it seemed as though it might be an hallucination but I followed the music and found its source. Paul was sitting on an upturned boat, one leg dangling nonchalantly over one side like a lonely, misplaced Pied-Piper. He was strumming the guitar gently and singing a folksy type of song. When he saw me approach he stopped singing but continued to strum the guitar.

'Leaving on the nineteenth of next month,' he spoke the words accompanied by his guitar. 'Two weeks early, good isn't it?' He continued playing. The rippling waters of the lagoon seemed to fit in with the gentle music as the waves softly lapped and caressed the sand. It soothed and relaxed.

'Used to play in a rock 'n' roll group,' Paul said, while he continued to play. 'Perhaps I'll join another band when I get demobbed in six months time. My three years are up then.' He accentuated the last statement with a glissando on the guitar. He continued playing. I sat on the sand. I leant against the hull of the boat and remained listening to the eloquent instrument; its lonely sound backed by the rhythm of the sea.

At 4.30 in the morning on Wednesday 27 June I was alone on night-shift fully recovered from the bout of exhaustion. Things were quiet so Bill had been stood down from duty. It was a hot, sticky night. It had been difficult to cat-nap for more than one or two hours so there had been no rude awakening by Mahatma who now announced the imminent advent of Bighorn.

There had been little interruption from the radio receiver and a long letter home was being completed. It explained that this was to be the largest bomb in the series. The letter would finish with a chronology of events about to take place. There was half an hour to go before Bighorn. The time was recorded in the letter. When D minus fifteen minutes was reached I paused after writing 'not long now,' and thought back to Jacky' s last letter; full of things about another place that was almost forgotten. They could have been a whole, not half, a world away.

Mahatma announced that there was a hold in the run and so the letter went on, 'It's been put back thirty minutes, that means there's time to cook breakfast. I'm hungry. It should be detonation at 6.00 am now.'

The countdown continued for another twenty minutes. Then there was yet another delay. It was as though the sheer size of Bighorn had made it slow, unwieldy and unwilling to come to fruition. The countdown recommenced and, finally, just before the last warnings, the dark goggles were put on.

This was the most vast and horrific energy flash of all. The initial daylight brilliance lasted for about two minutes; much longer than any of the other tests. The fireball, born at that moment, a stark speck from nothing grew rapidly larger. It continued to expand in silent, violent fury, as though it would never stop. It seemed that it could easily touch the island and then engulf the whole earth.

Looking at this spectacle through the window, it was easy to appreciate the size of the bomb. The letter was hastily picked up and I quickly left the radio cabin before the blast arrived. I stood on the hard coral some distance away and braced myself against what was certain to be one almighty explosion of noise and movement.

When it came, it was massive. The ground shook as though it were jelly. The vibration of the shock wave sent the cooking utensils on the outside table, crashing to the ground. Miraculously the radio cabin remained intact. It had seemed, as the earth shook, that the walls could easily have come tumbling down like a pack of cards.

As the rumble died down I gingerly walked back to the door of the radio cabin and stepped inside. The ceiling fan was still whirring unceasingly. Everything seemed to be in one piece apart from the wall clock which was lying on the floor.

The nuclear cloud now began to form. I wondered exactly how many megatons this bomb could have been. Before this it would have been impossible to contemplate anything greater, or more powerful, than those already witnessed. Bighorn had been aptly named. An obscene and monstrous shape formed gigantically in the sky. The

Port camp area remained lit for a long time in an eerie, orange, poisonous glow which emanated from its massive and unwelcome presence.

The size of Bighorn dominated the conversation for the rest of the day. Added to this were outside comments from the Hawaiian airwaves.

'This is KAPOI radio news desk. A thermo-nuclear device, exploded off Christmas Island today, was the most powerful yet in the current series of tests, having a yield of several megatons....'

'Putting it a bit mildly, aren't they?' Bill complained. 'Several megatons? I'd say it was e-fucking-normous!'

'Scared seven sorts of shit out of us,' added Paddy. 'That Sergeant shot out of his room when the blast came. He ran down the bloody beach like an olympic athlete.'

They were informed that the Sergeant was not the only one and that I had got out of the radio cabin pretty quick myself when the size of the bomb had become clear.

After Bighorn it was felt that the ultimate battering had been experienced. On Saturday 30 June, Mahatma warned of a following detonation but after Bighorn everyone knew the very worse that could be expected from any future bomb. The countdown continued hour upon hour. There was no stopping it. Then, once more, the most advanced of weaponry was put to test and bomb, number 22 was notched up to experience.

It was now the beginning of July and it was raining very hard. I stood underneath the verandah of the radio cabin, in four inches of water, cooking steak under the grill. Rain streamed from the gutterless, corrugated tin roof, like a waterfall. Beyond this aquatic curtain, there was nothing but total darkness. Alone, within the confines of the building, it felt like a prison. The silver, watery bars shimmered in the reflected light and I felt trapped, as though locked in some dark, magical cave, from which there was no escape.

Sitting on the outside step, breakfast was soon finished and I lit a cigarette. At home it would be four o'clock in the afternoon. It was easy to imagine an English summer's day; the light blue sky above dog roses in the hedge, strawberries with sugar and glasses of sweet wine underneath the rustle of apple trees. Although, perhaps it would be raining there as well and the hedge, shining green and dripping wet, would be confettied with rose petals that had fallen with the rain.

The last letter from Jacky had been short and unusually despairing. I sent flowers, through Interflora, via the NAAFI shop. News would eventually arrive at the radio cabin as it had done for several other servicemen but this one would be for me. The first, and probably last, personal message.

The shrill sound of morse code filled the cabin and my heart leapt in anticipation that this was the message. I jumped rapidly to give the response but it was just a routine signal and there was instant disappointment. The rain eased off with the first signs of daylight. The sun rose from beneath the horizon. It shone strongly through the haze to herald yet another steamy tropical day.

Jock came in to take over the shift. He busied himself with the first message. It contained some strange news.

'Would you believe it?' he asked incredulously. 'You remember that fellow who was raped and was sent home a couple of months back? Well that signal was asking for confirmation regarding his repatriation. At this point in time, he is being held in custody, as absent without leave.'

'Don't tell us they think the poor sod escaped?'

'Indeed it seems they do. I ask you, how in the hell in their pea-brained imagination, could anybody get off this island without any authority?'

'Not easy,' I replied, and it crossed my mind that, had it been possible, Jock would have done it by now.

'Well the short of it is,' Jock continued. 'He was at home awaiting further orders. He didn't hear anything so he decided to contact the records office in Gloucester to enquire about his new posting. Then they pulled him in. If it were me,' he went on, 'I would have stayed at home and waited for them to get in touch. Taken a long, extended leave. It's not his fault they can't sort out the stupid paper work when that's all they've got to do.'

Later on, one week into July, there was to be another test which, like Bighorn, was to receive its own special name from Mahatma. This was the test named 'Starfish Prime'. An H-bomb was to be detonated approximately 400 kilometres above the earth in the Van Allen Belt of the Earth's atmosphere. A Thor rocket would take the bomb up from Johnson Island.

On Sunday 7 July, the countdown for Starfish Prime bellowed out throughout the day. This detonation was to be carried out at night. Nobody knew what to expect because it was being carried out so far away but this time there was a direct role for us to play. Two of us on duty in the radio cabin were to monitor a series of signals sent from Fiji and Hawaii. This was to see the extent of interference with radio waves, during such a nuclear explosion. Protective glasses were unnecessary because of the distance involved.

The countdown continued until just past midnight, 'Five-four-three-two-one..'

Paddy and I wore earphones to monitor the two separate transmitters. We listened intently to our receivers and saw out of the cabin window that a sheet of white light had spread over an area of the dark, starry sky. It was confined to a high altitude and did not illuminate the island. It quickly ebbed, to be followed by an orange glow, like a sunset high in the heavens.

'Not much to get excited about,' Paddy commented, when everything had finished.

'You've been spoilt that's your trouble. You're not going to top Bighorn.'

We were to learn later that the population of Hawaii after they had witnessed the bomb had given their own name to Starfish Prime. They nicknamed it the 'Rainbow Bomb'.

Our one and only direct role in the test series was over. There was still no telegram with news from home. I began to feel worried. This found me spending more time than usual over at the radio cabin. It would make no difference to the outcome but would mean that I might receive any information immediately.

I stood outside the radio shack late in the evening and watched servicemen staggering back to their billets. On more than one occasion, the NAAFI bar had almost been 'drunk dry'. It was particularly evident that this might happen again.

More Americans had died, on the roads, bringing the total number now to 22. Bill stood by me, outside the communications centre, in sombre mood.

'What an epitaph!' he reflected. 'Death due to excess alcohol, smoking, Captain Flit's DDT spray, driving on the wrong side of the road, coral poisoning, eaten by sharks, radiation sickness, de-bloody-pression....'

Feeling on edge, I suggested to Bill that the night shift could be carried on without him and he sauntered back to the billet leaving me alone on duty. It was at times like this that I was pleased with my own company and, more importantly, I wanted to keep an ear in close proximity to the radio for the long awaited personal message.

There was no news during the night. On the way back to the billet I stubbed a toe painfully on a jagged lump of coral. This added to my feeling of depressed disappointment. I hobbled over to the shower block where I encouraged the cut to bleed and held it under the tap to make sure that every particle of coral sand was washed away. A grubby handkerchief was used to bind it up.

'You won't get medic-of-the-year award for that one,' Bill commented.

'Or the gunge I hope'

In fact, the cut healed surprisingly quickly without any sign of the dreaded coral poisoning which hospitalized many men during their stay on the island.

On Tuesday 10 July weary faces glanced at each other as they took their places on the beach of the lagoon to see the 24th detonation. Gone was any excited chatter or jocular quips. There was an atmosphere of 'Let's get it over with. We're sick of it'. There was no sign of the nervous Sergeant and it was later learned that he had been repatriated because his tour had finished. The countdown continued and the bomb appeared.

As before the enormous blast shook the surrounding area causing the ground to vibrate underfoot and Jock to exclaim, 'My nerves are shattered!'

There were no replies and everyone left the beach in silence.

'Last one's tomorrow morning, then,' said Bill, sounding pleased.

'Providing there are no delays,' John reminded him, also pointing out that they would leave on the 19 July if this bomb was on schedule.

'Special RAF Comet arriving on Thursday the 19th to take all extra personnel back home,' he said.

Bill greeted this idea by waving his arms about ecstatically and cheering with joy.

It was difficult for everyone else to share his enthusiasm although his departure represented another milestone that would bring us all nearer to the homeward run.

It was decided that a farewell barbecue should be held, in the area of the communications centre, on the evening of Thursday 12 July. The idea of this seemed to give everyone a much needed boost. It was a lift from the inexplicable tensions that had built up over the previous weeks and dried coconut husks were an ideal fuel. There were soon plenty of them piled high on a patch of coral adjacent to the radio cabin. Enough of the fuel was collected to ensure a long-lasting supply of glowing embers.

'This is Mahatma. This is Mahatma. D minus one hour. D minus one hour.'

Wednesday 11 July at 5.30 am. This really was to be the last one. Then it would be over. The tannoy's familiar raucous sound aroused me but I felt too tired to move out of bed. The first thought was that the telegram had not yet arrived from home. The baby had not been born. It seemed as though there would be no more birth, just an angel of death lurking in a nuclear cloud. I drifted back to sleep which came and went throughout the countdown.

Emerging from this state the lifeless shapes of my companions became visible. The light from the false dawn lit the room in stark light and black shadow, but they did not stir. Then came the nerve racking resonance of the detonation shaking the wooden walls. Sound exploded round the room. Tired faces began to appear from under the wrinkled sheets.

'Missed the last one,' Paddy yawned. 'No more megaton bloody mornings.'

The following day the Section Warrant Officer collected the film badges and goggles.

'How do you know who owned what?' he was asked as they were handed to him. 'They're not even labelled or anything.'

'Search me,' he replied, with a world-weary tone in his voice.

He held a film badge aloft. 'I don't even know how they are supposed to work. If they do.'

'It's just as well,' John said, cynically. 'The main thing is, the bombs did.'

CHAPTER FIFTEEN

Goodbye Mahatma - Hello Hawaii

Extra steaks were purloined from the airmen's mess for the barbecue. It was meant to be a farewell party for the handful of airmen connected with signals who were about to return to the United Kingdom. It was fortunate that the amount of food needed had been overestimated because some of the guests had little, or no, connection with the signals section. It must have been the unusual sight of a bonfire that attracted attention; it drew the curious, like moths to a lamp. The padre who had been invited, paid a visit, it was well known that he was not averse to a pint of beer.

The Section Officer brought a few of his fellow officers but they did not stay long. He seemed to make it clear that he felt more comfortable with our company. During the course of the evening we got him to verify that his father was a Member of Parliament. Jock thought he would test the extent of his influence.

'Couldn't your father bring any authority to bear and get us all off this bloody island?' he asked.

'He's not the Minister of Defence you know,' the Officer replied.

'Pity, I thought we were on to a winner,' came Jock's unsurprised response.

Burnt meat covered in white, powdery ash was handed round by a volunteer from the cookhouse who had elected to act as chef for the occasion.

'Probably the first time he's ever cooked anything,' John commented, critically turning over and examining the scorched meat.

'Nah!' Bill replied, charitably. 'I bet he's done it before. He's just pissed.'

'Aren't we all,' observed Paddy over the chunk of over-cooked beef that he was trying to bite through.

As the evening went on men gradually wandered away from the celebrations, returning either singly or in small groups to their billets. The heap of burning husks grew lower and glowed less brightly. The barbecue finally came to an end late in the evening when the beer ran out. The space beside the communications centre became deserted. All that remained of the fire was the patch of dying embers which made a dull orange-black stain on the light grey dust. Depression returned.

Shortly after the evening of the barbecue Paddy managed to escape for a short spell. His additional qualifications allowed him to make an exchange with Hickam. This left Jock and I to say farewell to the happy-go-lucky Paul. Paul passed on ownership of the boat with the patched sail before he went. Then he bade an ecstatic goodbye to the island. The very last sight of him was a glimpse of fair, wavy hair, bleached ever lighter by the sun, together with the guitar slung nonchalantly across one shoulder. The guitar looked strangely out of place against the khaki military uniform that he wore.

Thursday 19 July was the day that all the extra personnel left the island for good. They were the lucky ones. There was also a funeral on that day. It was for a Royal Navy rating, who had died from 'accidental causes'. He was buried at sea just beyond the reef. A volley of rifle shots echoed around the Port Area and the body was lowered into the deep blue waters of the Pacific. During the evening a special service was held for those who wished to pay their last respects. A plaque was attached to the wall of the chapel, for yet another man that the place would not let go.

This latest tragedy, together with those American deaths we had heard about, made a total of 25 men killed. It was almost as if the island demanded immediate payment, for what had happened, and wanted to keep an exact share of human sacrifice. The tally was 25 hydrogen bombs tested and 25 men dead.

John and Bill now boarded the RAF coach, headed for the airfield and home.

'It won't be long before you're both off this bloody rock,' Bill said encouragingly.

'Been nice knowing you,' said John. 'Sorry we can't stay,' he added, unconvincingly.

'Why rush off, then?' I laughed.

'Gotta plane to catch,' John replied happily.

The coach pulled away, leaving a trail of dust in its wake. Jock looked longingly down the road after it.

'Lucky devils!' he said, shrugging his shoulders. 'Well, I don't mind admitting it, I think I'll miss them.'

Immediately after the bus had left, I went over to the radio cabin to find out whether the telegram had arrived. It had still not come. The anxious feeling crept over me, once more. Jacky's letters arrived regularly. She wrote every day but because of the distance letters arrived in small batches, some five days after posting. The latest one just stated that the baby was overdue and a nurse was looking after her. I wondered whether everything was all right. It was frustrating - waiting so far away. It occupied my mind for much of the time and I tried to I console myself with the idea that if anything really went wrong I would be told quite quickly.

The Section Officer came out of his small office at the back of the radio cabin.

'Chas you haven't had your leave in Hawaii yet have you? Everyone needs a break from this place. You're entitled to six day's leave and you won't be allowed to get away from the island any earlier by not taking it. Look, get on the Hastings tomorrow. Don't worry about the telegram. We'll make sure it finds you in Hawaii.'

And so on the following day I found myself on a plane bound for Hawaii.

There were six on board the Hastings when it took to the air early Friday morning. It felt strange wearing shoes and socks for the first time in months. They made the feet feel uncomfortable and totally cramped. I kept removing them and then putting them back on again throughout the five and a half hour journey to Honolulu. Strangely enough considering the small size of the British service community on the island my travelling companions did not know each other but everyone had introduced themselves by the time the flight was over and it was established that everybody would be staying at the American servicemen's rest centre, Fort de Russy, which was situated near Waikiki Beach,

The plane touched down at Honolulu International Airport amid huge commercial airliners and taxied down to the far end, reserved for military aircraft. We stepped off the Hastings and walked towards a small group of buildings reserved for the RAF detachment stationed there. The easily recognizable outline of Brian came out to greet us.

'Welcome to Hickam, Chas. Bet you're glad to get off that bloody island for a while?'

'Are you kidding! I want to go back there - feel homesick for it already.'

I tried to look serious but he laughed and said that he had the afternoon off and would accompany us to Fort de Russy. After that, we could look around the town. Brian led the way to a large Chevrolet taxi which contained a massively genial Hawaiian driver behind its steering wheel. The seven men slipped into the long, sleek car with plenty of room to spare.

Fort de Russy was set amongst luxurious hotels. It was, as they would say in glossy brochures, only a few minutes walk from the famous Waikiki beach. At any other time in my life the wide bay would have been impressive. It was an expanse of sparkling blue water with safe bathing, where surf riders skimmed and soared atop white crested waves. Native outriggers, packed with wide-eyed tourists, weaved their way from one side of the bay to the other. Concrete hotels, gleaming white in the sun, edged onto sands which were packed with thousands of people. However, although I was loathe to admit it, the desolate white coral sands of Christmas Island had a far more exotic visual appeal. They were untamed, a place where a seething ocean crashed against deserted beaches, edged with green topped coconut palms, swaying and bowing to the wild blue Pacific. Waikiki must have looked like that many years ago.

The accommodation for servicemen was cheap; only one dollar per night, with three sharing a room. It took a little while to get adjusted to the hustle and bustle of civilian life. The main avenue was a busy thoroughfare edged with tamed, stiff, palm trees placed at regimented intervals alongside rows of parking meters. Crossing the road was hectic for someone whose experience with heavy traffic had been allowed to lapse and it took some time before we lost the feeling of being nomads out of the desert who had just arrived in the confusing big city.

Shorts, gaily printed Hawaiian style shirts and heavy tans made it possible to blend immediately, like brown chameleons, into the cosmopolitan lifestyle of the place. The only time any curiosity was shown towards us was when our accents provoked comment. Guesses as to our origin ranged from Boston to Australia and New Zealand but never England. It was inconceivable that the English would turn up in the middle of the Pacific without wearing bowler hats!

As interesting as it was, Honolulu was not at all what had been expected. It was not a native paradise but a cosmopolitan commercial centre. People lying on Waikiki beach never seemed to touch the sand but always lay on mats which were carried with them when they left, tucked under their arms.

At the International Market Place we stopped and watched some girls in sarongs rehearsing a hula dance. They were being put through their paces by a thin, miserable looking man with rolled up sleeves. Most of the girls were more Chinese looking than Polynesian. They were slick and slim like any other dancing troupe being trained at a small-town provincial theatre. I thought back to the Gilbertese dancers who ranged from very young girls to much older women who took their dance so seriously and would not dance for money.

At one point in the tour we came face to face with a seedy looking oriental man.

'You guys wanna woman?' he spat out in a strange Chinese-American accent. He stood there for a moment, nervously looking us up and down.

The group of young men looked at each other and answered in unison, 'Eh?'

The timing was perfect; the surprise had been genuine and loud.

The idea of women being 'served up on a plate' was astonishingly alien. The man backed away, as though he were being confronted by people from another planet. As he went he called back, 'You guys forget it!'

The shadowy figure quickly scurried off and disappeared from sight, into the depths of a side-street.

'What did he want?' asked the youngest member of the group, who was about nineteen and from the north of England.

'He was a pimp,' I informed him, wondering at the same time whether he had really not heard or whether

Newcastle did not offer much by way of education in the seamier side of life.

It seemed as though in this place they had put the Garden of Eden up for auction - although, paradoxically, paradise was not exactly what they had for sale. Brian was surprised by my reaction to Honolulu and Waikiki. We sat in the Davy Jones Locker bar and watched swimmers in a glass sided pool swim past, like fish in a tank. I said I thought that, while other parts of Hawaii were probably beautiful and more natural, this part seemed a bit like a twentieth century concrete pleasure boat serving much the same purpose that Southend or Brighton served for Edwardian London.

'You must have gone native! I thought you were a city boy? Don't tell me you'd rather be in Southend!'

He made me feel like a homing bird or a salmon that always swims upstream to its birthplace. It was hard to explain why but as much as the bustle of Honolulu was enjoyable I would rather have been back home.

My desire to be in England lay with people more than place and on Monday 23 July the long-awaited telegram at last arrived.

Brian phoned the news from Hickam to the hotel at Fort de Russy. He read out over the telephone, 'BOY BORN 20TH JULY STOP MOTHER AND BABY FINE STOP.' Then he added, 'It's been around a bit, you know. Paddy has just taken it down from Christmas Island. He sends his congratulations. It came via Fiji, Singapore and the rest. Congratulations Chas.'

It was a boy! A feeling of total joy erupted through me. I walked through the town that day and passed the multi-coloured shops, the busy bars and the cafes lining the Main Avenue and Honolulu was transformed. The world seemed a marvellous place once more.

CHAPTER SIXTEEN

New moons and Tongareva.

Things were very different on Christmas Island when I returned. Weary from travel I lay on top of the bed with eyes closed. The silence, after hours of listening to the constant drone of the Hastings engines on the return flight, was emphatic. Then it seemed as though there was something wrong. I was tense and on edge, as though waiting for something to happen. Something was missing. Gradually the realization dawned that I was waiting to be alerted by Mahatma's piercing tones. I sat up and looked out of the window. The all-pervasive tannoy had gone; it must have been taken down in the past week. I lay back and closed my eyes again. This time every muscle was relaxed.

Over the weeks that followed new faces began to appear to take the place of those who had left. Their white skins gained a colour which gradually became deeper and deeper as the days passed. Jock was fascinated by one whom he referred to as a 'bit of a character'. This made me wonder what strange kind of eccentric could have come to join us until Jock explained that he collected shells.

'Well, what's wrong with that?' I queried.

'Nothing really but I was walking along the beach with him the other day and I just happened to tread on a bloody shell...'

'That does tend to happen all the time, surely?' I interrupted.

'Exactly,' Jock smiled. 'Anyhow the short of it is I thought he was going to have a heart attack or something. It was the type that he'd been searching for since he'd arrived. I left him there holding the pieces together. He's been spending his spare time looking for another since.'

Jock looked as though he found such an interest incomprehensible. I felt it would be quite interesting to see what the man had already found but Jock summed it all up with the comment, 'He must be shell-shocked!'

Stranger still to us, and even more incomprehensible, was another new arrival. This man from the start greeted the island as a haven. To him it was some kind of deliverance. He was actually pleased to arrive there!

Paddy had returned from his exchange posting and we all listened incredulously as the happy-go-lucky airman, with flashing eyes and a permanent grin, revealed his story.

'You think you've had problems?' he said. 'How about this then? Two years ago I was serving in Hong Kong and married a Chinese girl. We had two kids. We got posted back home but then we lived apart for a while and I found a girlfriend. Just before I got posted out here, the girlfriend tells me she's pregnant. Now, when I get back in 48 week's time my girlfriend's two massive brothers will either want a marriage or a murder. They don't know I'm already married.'

'Jesus!' Paddy sympathized between his teeth. 'What a state to get into.'

'I know, I know,' the man replied, smiling at his own misfortune.

'That's why I'm not too bothered about being here. At least I can't get into any more trouble.'

'I bet your letters are interesting, assuming both your wife and girlfriend know you're here,' I commented.

'Oh, they know I'm here all right. They found out from my last station. I got two letters come together the other day; one from each of them. Neither knows about the other.'

'That's one consolation,' Paddy said.

'For how long?' I added.

With a grin and a shrug of his broad shoulders, he said, 'Who knows? At least while I'm here I have some breathing space.'

With that the airman left the room.

'Disgusting,' Paddy muttered.

'What is?' I said, surprised at Paddy's comment because he had seemed to relish the man's exploits.

'The fact that he isn't bothered about being posted here. That's what is really disgusting.'

On the whole the island was beginning to acquire a more serious clientele altogether. Warning went out that the medical officer was one of this fresh breed. Unfortunately I had to go and see him. My limbs had been aching and had felt stiff for some time and the advice was to go and have a check up.

At the sick bay a medical orderly in a long white coat, was stationed at a desk waiting to greet patients. On hearing the problem he said that it was probably due to the lack of salt. The medical orderly then decided that his diagnosis should be confirmed and asked me to wait a few minutes. He entered a room adjacent to his desk and after a while he called out that it was all right to enter the room.

The medical officer was standing up scanning through a book. His neatly pressed, gleaming white unbuttoned coat bore his officer's rank at the shoulder. His untanned face confirmed that he was new to the island. I decided that rumours about his total lack of humour could be put to test.

After a cold, brisk examination with his stethoscope he asked curtly, 'Been here long?'

'No, sir, I've only just walked in.'

He hesitated jerkily for a moment, glanced disinterestedly out of the window, and said, 'I meant on the island.'

'Oh,' I replied, in feigned innocence. 'Since last November.'

He made a quick note on his pad and asked automatically, 'Have you been here before?'

'No, sir. In fact this is my first overseas posting.'

Again he hesitated, glanced at the orderly as though he considered it a pity that he had to deal with congenital idiots, sighed and said, 'I meant have you visited sick quarters before?'

'Yes, sir.'

'When?' he asked quickly and sharply.

'At my last posting in the UK.'

He bit his lower lip and repeated, slowly, 'Have you ever visited this sick bay before?'

'Yes, sir.'

'Ah!' He seemed pleased. 'What for?'

'To visit a friend that got sunburnt.'

The orderly walked towards the door excusing himself, his eyes betraying a stifled amusement. The medical officer looked up from his pad. Unsmiling, he stared at me long and hard. 'They're right; no sense of humour,' I thought. 'This shouldn't have been started.' Eventually, he looked out of the window and said ponderously but precisely, 'Have you any other complaints?' Then before there was a chance to answer he quickly added, 'No, no, no, what I mean is - have you suffered from any other form of illness since you arrived on this island?'

He had called it to a halt.

'No, sir,' I admitted.

'Good. It seems that you are lacking salt. I would suggest that you take one or two extra salt tablets at meal times. They are freely available are they not?'

'Yes, sir.'

He looked suspicious as he said, 'That'll be all.'

On my way out the laughing medical orderly informed me, 'He doesn't like piss-takers does he?'

'Neither do I. It's a filthy habit.'

The orderly continued laughing until his superior suddenly appeared in the doorway to glare at both of us, before retreating back into his antiseptic realm.

While the new faces became more familiar we watched how they adapted and got used to their new surroundings; what their reactions were to an environment that we now took so much for granted. They were foreseeable and anticipated. One spat out tea in disgust when a dead chit-chat lizard came bobbing up to the surface. Faces creased in disbelief at the discovery of 'weirdies' in the bread. Familiar errors were made like filling the kettle from the tap used only for washing floors; we would then find ourselves taking a sip of tea made from salt water straight from the lagoon.

The newcomers were to enjoy a little more comfort than some of the island's previous occupants. Eventually everyone was issued with interior sprung mattresses. The Station Warrant Officer called into the billet to give a delivery time and was very surprised to find that our interior sprung mattresses had already been acquired; that the beds in our billet were already up to standard as far as comfort was concerned.

He left the room with a puzzled, 'Give this place a bit of a dust out, will you?' as though this was a phrase that was etched into his memory.

There was only one more sight of him after this, and that was on the day of his departure.

When the Station Warrant Officer left the island he looked fit and strong. There was no trace of the gunge and no sign of the bandages that had adorned his limbs for most of the time. The reason behind the bound legs and slight permanent limp was finally unearthed. Just before he left we discovered that they were due to an injury he had suffered in World War Two. He had bailed out from a stricken Lancaster bomber and his parachute had failed to deploy properly.

The Station Warrant Officer approached the door of the coach and turned. The deeply tanned face was beaming and he surveyed the scene around him for one last time. There was no doubt about it he looked a credit to himself and to Muscle Beach.

Then as though to mark a pointer which, at last, would put me closer to my own homeward run, the time came for Jock to leave. Jock's farewell began early - too early. It was Sunday lunchtime in the NAAFI. He was plied with drinks from all directions. Paddy and I left the bar to the sounds of Jock singing and playing the piano for all he was worth.

Later that afternoon it was not surprising to see him staggering down the road, towards the billet. A passing airman, a recent arrival, made a derogatory remark about Jock's condition. The reaction was swift and lucid.

'Who are you calling pissed? Get some bloody time in!'

The airman scampered away, not wishing to remain the subject of Jock's strong riposte. He entered the room and sat heavily on his bed.

'I suppose this evening's celebrations are now cancelled,' I remarked.

'I couldn't touch another drop,' he sighed, turned and flopped, face down, on his pillow.

At 8.30 am on the next morning, 27 August, Jock was up, dressed and ready to leave, showing the usual signs of astounding recovery. Paddy and I accompanied him to the waiting blue coach.

We shook hands and he said, 'Give us a look up, if you are ever in Scotland some day.'

'Yes, of course,' I replied.

We watched the coach drive off, churning mounds of coral from the rear wheels until it was out of sight swallowed by the dust in its wake.

'It'll seem strange without that big lug here, won't it?' Paddy remarked.

At the same time as the visible changes occurred at Port Camp those taking place at Main Camp were even more marked. On a last visit to the American stronghold, we sat in the massive cinema watching *The King and I*. There was only a handful of men scattered here and there in the tiered seats. The Surf Club was also depressingly empty and devoid of the vigorous and energetic life it once knew.

'The whole place is getting like a ghost town,' the barman volunteered.

It looked as though the island was about to claim Main Camp back for its own. It would become the deserted, rusted collection of buildings that it had been before the Americans arrived. Brigadoon was slowly disappearing into the mists of time.

It was on this last sight of Main Camp, that an uneasy doubt crept into my thinking. It was all too simple; the bombs had finished, the area was being evacuated. Was that the end to the matter? Why had the tests been brought forward in the first place? For what reason had we been kept on the island for such minimal involvement? There seemed to be a vague question of threat which was to remain until the dramatic events which were to unfold some weeks later.

At the present time though all was quiet. The main contingent of US servicemen had left but we learnt that the Americans were still making regular trips to Tongareva, a small coral atoll south of the Equator. The word went out that any time they had spare room they would take extra passengers along with them.

When we asked what we could do in Tongareva, we were told, 'Barter. The natives love bartering. Old clothes are the best thing to take with you. You can swop 'em for model boats, grass skirts - even pearls.'

'Pearls?' I echoed.

We were shown a matchbox which contained four pearls carefully wrapped in cotton wool.

'The natives are fantastic swimmers, they dive for them. You can't get the best ones - there's a Pearl Commission there - but, at least, they're real.'

'What did you give for them?'

'An old khaki shirt.'

Paddy and I decided to arrange a booking on the next trip. On the 26 September we boarded a giant American transport aircraft bound for Tongareva, or Penryn as it was also known; an island owned jointly by New Zealand and the United States.

We sat in the massive cargo bay where the space was dominated by a big yellow bulldozer. As this giant of the skies made its way down the runway it seemed as though it would be a miracle if it were to become airborne. Doubts were ill-founded and it inched its way skyward.

Coffee was an on-going thing; there was an invitation to come up to the cockpit whenever refreshment was needed. The navigator was asked how far it was to Tongareva.

'Bout 750 miles due south,' he told us. 'Should be a six hour round trip.'

The previous day all unwanted items of clothing had been gathered together to use for bartering. Piles of surplus shirts and shorts had been accumulated by the ten RAF servicemen on board.

From the cockpit of the aircraft the island came into view. It was a thin white ring of coral with a light green emerald centre surrounded by a deep blue sea. Scattered around the island were smooth, white, oval shapes of coral lying just below the surface of the water.

The aircraft made its approach and flew just above tree-top height down the centre of the runway. It then gained height, banked and turned to make another approach.

'Have to make sure there's nothing blocking the runway,' explained the navigator. 'There's no such thing as air traffic control down there.'

Wheels came into contact with the hard coral surface. Engines roared and brakes were applied. The plane shook and bumped its way along until it finally came to a halt at the opposite end of the runway.

By the time we had disembarked the aircraft was surrounded by smiling, friendly Maoris. They were waving and chattering excitedly. They had clasped by their bronzed bodies various articles which they had made themselves. These were to be traded for the cast-off items of clothing.

Within minutes all my old clothes had been exchanged for various items. A shirt was swapped for a model boat fashioned like a native outrigger. It was made from coconut palm wood, inlaid with decorations of mother-of-pearl. Another shirt paid for a grass skirt. The skirt was made from a stiff rounded grass attached to a brightly coloured belt which was woven in typical, colourful, geometric, Maori patterns. Shorts paid for fans made from oyster shells edged with dyed grasses. By the time the bartering had finished, I had acquired three imperfect but real pearls, glowing with ambiguous colour; these would be for Jacky.

The Maoris spoke very little English to us but they remained within the vicinity of the aircraft throughout its two hour stay on the airstrip. The land on this part of the island was no more than two hundred yards wide. This could be clearly seen by looking across the runway. From the air the island had been seen as a narrow ring around a central lagoon. This circular strip was about 25 miles round.

'Must be a funny way of life here,' Paddy observed. 'Like living on a giant ring. Whichever way you go you'll end up where you started.'

Coconut palms grew in abundance and in the distance, were some native dwellings. They were similar in appearance to those in the Gilbertese village of London on Christmas Island.

An airman struggled by with a heavy turtle shell which must have measured about three feet across.

'Make a decent ashtray,' someone commented to him as he passed by them with his load.

Then attention was drawn to the sound of music which was coming from one corner of the airstrip. A small group of girls had started to sing. One of them sat on the ground, playing an accompaniment on what appeared to be a miniature ukulele. Closer inspection revealed that the instrument was fashioned from a half-coconut shell. The scooped out shell had been connected to a flat piece of palm wood to which tunable strings were attached. The soft sound that was produced resembled a muffled ukulele.

She finished playing. The other girls stopped their singing and she offered the coconut ukulele for trade. It was a marvellous instrument but the airman with the giant shell was the first to step forward. The exchange was made and he placed the ukulele inside his turtle shell, before walking back towards the aircraft to store them away.

Paddy then noticed four other girls who had climbed into a Jeep. They attempted to start the engine like children playing with a toy. They squealed happily as the vehicle lurched forward and they repeated the game several times, before the owner came forward and removed the keys. He did this with a friendly wagging of his finger and they smiled joyfully at him, their eyes rolling with amusement.

Their attention was then attracted to Paddy. He was smiling at them. They nudged each other and began giggling. Then, gathering together one or two others, they made a spontaneous attempt at a hula dance for us. It was a rather ramshackle affair; they moved awkwardly and giggled. They sometimes looked down at their bare feet as their hips swung within loose-fitting cotton dresses. They were wearing circles of flowers on their heads and one girl's garland slipped down. It got caught on one side over her ear. They collapsed into laughter but after a while regained their composure to some extent and went on to continue the show with joyful enthusiasm.

Then they decided to pose for photographs with us. They pulled us in line with them, patted our uniforms and pushed our caps over our eyes, then placed their arms around our necks and waists, playfully nudging us whenever we tried to stand steady. They seemed to wind themselves warmly against us and each other as though they were always used to being tied in a human ring on their tiny island. Paddy looked very young and very happy.

A young Maori man stepped forward and seriously beckoned me to photograph him. When the film had been taken he immediately offered me a wooden fan that he had made.

'I have nothing left to exchange for it,' I said slowly.

He answered in halting English, 'That alright,' and he pushed the fan towards me.

I fumbled in my pockets and produced a few coins. I knew that he could not spend them on the island but even so had the idea that perhaps they could be put to some use. He took them and then pointed to a small woman standing nearby.

'My mother. Take picture?' he said moving towards her. She looked too young and delicate to be his mother. His massive frame dwarfed hers as they stood side by side posing whilst I ran some cine film.

'He'd make two of us,' Paddy commented.

'Must be a healthy life here,' I said, examining the fan that he had given to me and noting how dried grass had been threaded through holes around the edge. The mother-of-pearl swirling with colour had been set into the surface on one side.

We asked the Maori how many years he had been on the island.

'Seventeen,' came the reply.

'You were born here?'

'Yes. Born here.'

He may have been born on this ringed island but his strength and stature made him look more as though he belonged to the vast ocean rather than to this small stretch of land.

At that point the call was made for us to board the aircraft. The time had passed very quickly but the islanders remained waving as the aircraft turned round and commenced its take off. Lightened of its cumbersome load the plane seemed to take to the sky more readily than before. Within a little over three hours the southern tip of Christmas Island came back into view.

CHAPTER SEVENTEEN

Cuba and the grapefruit run

The giant transport plane flew over the southern part of Christmas Island on its return from Tongareva. Here the vegetation was sparse and it came to mind that this was probably the old A-bomb testing site that had been used in the 1950's. Paddy had come to the same conclusion.

'I wonder if it's still radioactive down there?' he said, as we passed over the sad and barren looking area.

We landed and arrived back at the billet around six in the evening. The mail had arrived during the day and amongst the letters was one from Jock. The news was that he had renewed his pilot's licence. The correspondence went on to say that he had been staying with his sister. He reckoned that his blood must have 'thinned out' because he was feeling extremely cold. We remembered back to the letters he received from his sister during his stay on the island. She had always maintained that the Highland deer were a great deal happier while he was away. There were scars on Jock's chest, inflicted by a charging stag, which verified her opinion. This led us all to wonder how uneasy the herds might be feeling, now.

The weeks that followed passed uneventfully. The only general excitement, was that generated by the arrival of the long-awaited plate wash. The tin trays could at last be discarded. A new army barber also caused something of a stir. There was a general unofficial warning not to visit him before leaving the island, with such comments as, 'Bloke's in the wrong trade - should have been a carpenter. The old joke about needing an anaesthetic - it truly applies to that butcher!'

It was discovered during those last few weeks that the island could manage to influence even the most unlikely of its customers. This realization came on a second visit to the medical officer to find out the cause of the slight chest pains that I had been suffering. The medical officer was in the same room but this time he was sitting back looking relaxed and heavily tanned. He was accompanied by the same grinning orderly. I made no attempt at any jokes; reminding myself that the man had no sense of humour. After a thorough examination however he pronounced that the condition was the same as the one that he had suffered from ever since he had arrived on the island.

'It's the crap food that causes it,' he proclaimed.

'Well, I've never had it before.'

'Well, you've got it now.'

He looked almost gleeful as he poured a measure of liquid into a container, 'Here, drink this,' he ordered.

I gulped down the liquid. 'Good stuff, that,' I said. His gleeful look had made me feel somewhat defensive.

'You're not supposed to enjoy it,' he replied, smiling. When I left, I wondered whether this was the same doctor as the one I had seen earlier.

There was to be one more nuclear test. This took place on Friday 19 October. It was carried out from Johnson Island and was detonated, 200 or more miles high, in the Van Allen Belt. Due to the distance involved and, probably, the time of day, there was nothing to be seen or heard of it.

Then came the news that my replacement was arriving. He was due on the island by the third week of October. I was elated. It seemed certain now that I would be home by the end of the month. However no repatriation date was given to me. The itinerary of my replacement was followed with avid interest. Each step was registered as he journeyed half way round the world. He finally arrived on an RAF Comet IV on the date that had been expected. Even so there was still no repatriation confirmation for me.

At first I had been filled with excitement. Now doubts began to creep into my mind. It was hard to join in the customary wild and enthusiastic reception for the newcomers. There was no certainty for me. Others had been allowed to leave the island as much as three weeks early. The Comet was due to leave in two days time, one or two others were to return on it but I was not booked on that flight.

Then on the 22 October came some unbelievable news. It came through on one of the Hawaiian radio stations. The news was that the President of the United States, JF Kennedy, had placed a naval 'quarantine' on Cuba.

The communist country of Cuba had been a thorn in the side of the United States since the Americans had supported the unsuccessful Bay of Pigs invasion by Cuban anti-communist refugees. Soviet Chairman, Nikita Krushchev, promised to defend Cuba with Russian arms. Medium and intermediate-range ballistic missiles were to be installed in Cuba. Krushchev had calculated that the Bay of Pigs embarrassment would prevent America from lifting a finger to prevent the threat on her doorstep.

In July 1962 the Soviet Union began missile shipments to Cuba; a third world country with a dictator at its head. It was like sending grenades to a kindergarten. In the following month American U2 spy planes flying over Cuba reported the presence of Soviet technicians as well as new military construction on the missile site. In Cuba, on 14 October 1962, a ballistic missile sat ready and threatening, on a launching site, at the edge of the North American continent. It was then that Kennedy took action. He announced that the United States would seize any offensive weapons, and associated material, that Soviet vessels might try to deliver to Cuba.

Now came the time to wait and see. What would happen if, or when, the Russian ships moved across the ocean and met with the American Navy? If this were to happen war would be inevitable. For those of us who had seen the tests it was impossible to picture the teaming countries of Europe, America and Russia embroiled in nuclear war. The mayhem, suffering and destruction was unthinkable. The bombs that had just been tested were not small atom bombs, like those that had been used twice before, terrible though they were. They were poison mega-giants; they killed in hundreds of square miles by the thousands and left death to hover on for generations.

'Probably cancelled due to war,' was Paddy's grim comment when I started to wonder aloud about the reason why I had not yet been given a repatriation date. Doubts swamped my mind. I saw again the London of my childhood; the shattered streets and torn houses, the waste, the faces of brave, but tired and tormented, people. I began to wonder whether I would ever see my wife and children again.

So the world held its breath. I held mine. A week went by. Messages were exchanged between Kennedy and Krushchev. The US Navy began to move into position. The impossible was happening. The United States was now preparing for war.

Then on 28 October a message came from Krushchev. He informed Kennedy that work on the Cuban missile sites would be halted. The missiles would be brought back from Cuba. Krushchev admitted that they were offensive, surface to surface, medium and intermediate range weapons. Russia slipped back from the careless brink. She returned her bombs to more local storage. The 'Great Powers' retreated, like misers putting lethal vipers along with their wealth back into a box for someone else to open in the future.

It was over. The Cuba crisis had eased. One week before my year on the island had been completed, news of the repatriation date arrived and I was on the 'grapefruit run'.

'Grapefruit run?' questioned my replacement, when he was gleefully told the news.

'The last meal you have here is breakfast. Grapefruit is only ever served at breakfast time. So, once you've had the grapefruit you know you're on the way.'

It was at this point that a Warrant Officer gave us the information that the American Air Force had traced one of their missing refrigerators to our radio cabin.

'Well, it was a sort of a loan so to speak,' I told him. 'Are they going to ship the lot off the island?'

'Don't know,' said the Warrant Officer. 'Anyway, we had better make sure it's clean and ready for them by the end of the week; that's when they said they would send a truck to pick it up.'

The refrigerator was emptied regretfully. It was cleaned up until it gleamed like new, ready for its owners to retrieve.

'That's cocked up the cold beer and raw ration storage,' said Paddy as he contemplated our handiwork. 'Things are not going to be the same.'

On Monday 5 November 1962, I looked around the room that had been home for the past twelve months. Nothing much seemed to have changed since I first set eyes on it. The same pictures smiled down from the wall and the furniture was unchanged. The only slight differences were that mattresses had been updated, the tin trays were no longer in view and it was *my* 'chuff' chart that hung on the wall. I gave a final glimpse towards where it remained firmly attached in its place above my bed and then I closed the door.

Paddy was on hand to help with one of the suitcases. At 7.30 am the bus was already parked outside the airmen's mess.

'Doesn't look as though you'll have many travelling companions,' he remarked, looking at the five solitary looking figures spaced out on the bus.

'As long as I'm going, that's the main thing.'

'Know what you mean,' Paddy replied and then, as an afterthought, 'By the way, did you pick up a packed lunch from the mess?'

'Yes, made sure it was hand picked. No wierdie sandwiches for me.'

We shook hands and I boarded the bus. The driver was already seated and within seconds the vehicle pulled out of the Port Area.

No-one said much throughout the journey to the airfield. I was content to sit back and watch the morning sun; to see it rise and flicker through the palm leaves that were swaying lazily in the breeze. The realization began to dawn that, at last, this was the first leg of the journey home.

At the airfield a sergeant checked off names. My route had been chosen because it was a fast one. He took me to one side and said, 'You'll leave Honolulu tomorrow morning on a BOAC Boeing 707 bound for San Francisco, Idlewild-New York and then Heathrow-London. By the way, wear civvies on that kite, okay?'

It was obvious that the others were merely going on leave to Hawaii and that there would be enough time to say goodbye to Brian at Hickam. This would be one time that I would feel more fortunate than he.

The Hastings charged down the runway and took to the skies. The pilot banked and turned the aircraft as he set course for the Hawaiian Islands. I felt compelled to have one last look at Christmas Island. Peering through the dusty porthole I surveyed the Port Camp area, the large lagoon and tiny Cook Island at the mouth of the reef. I remained looking at the curved line of the beach, edged with rows of white waves which crashed against it, until I saw only ocean and the island was no more. Then, removing my shoes, I shook out the last remnants of coral sand, sat back and relaxed.

Three days later the Boeing 707 touched down in London amid swirls of mist and fog. In a last minute decision the Captain had decided that it was safe to land at Heathrow and had not diverted to Birmingham.

It was 9.30 in the evening and there was plenty of time to catch a train at Fenchurch Street Station. Things had changed at the station. The hissing steam engines and the acrid smell of burning coal had gone. Electrification of the railway line had been completed during my absence. The place had changed and so had I.

The new train made the journey much faster than the old steam train would have done but in the poor conditions little could be seen from its windows. Only rows of city terraced homes and their sea of chimneys could be made out close to the railway line. As the train moved out of the town a swirling blackness lay outside and it was an almost unfamiliar reflected face that stared back at me from the carriage window. The fog grew denser the nearer the train got to the coast and to the end of the line.

The train journey had taken only a half hour or so. I now stepped out of the taxi, that had brought me from Benfleet Station. The fog wrapped itself around me, like a cold, damp blanket. I felt muffled, independent and isolated; an individual very separate from the rest of the world.

The privet hedge in front of the house loomed up ahead. I passed through the gate and cold drops of water from the hedge brushed along the side of my face and slid down into my neck. A light was shining softly through the mist.

Not a day had passed when I had not yearned for her. The 'warrior' had ended his wanderings. He had seen the kind of monsters that have always lurked deep in man's mythology and knew that they had been real. But at that moment it was the simplest thing that seemed most difficult. Warrior-hero-returned, maybe, but now I paused to wonder if I even knew how to say 'hello'.

EPILOGUE

Twenty years after the events described in this book Jacky and I spent a holiday touring Scotland. Gradually, we pushed further north to reach Cape Wrath on the extreme northwest coast where Jacky had stayed for a short time as a small child during one of her father's wartime RAF postings.

This goal accomplished, the possibility of locating Jock was considered. The only clue I had was that he lived in the area of Fort William. Communities are small in the surrounding country and local enquiries led to his brother. He in turn was able to provide an address and Jock was finally located in a small Highland town. Needless to say much reminiscing was done. Jock had received a medical discharge from the RAF in 1963. His premature release did not however attract a disability pension. His condition was, as in so many other cases, purported to be 'unrelated to service'.

Up to this point Christmas Island had, to me, remained buried in the past. Little seemed to be known by most of my contemporaries either about the island or British involvement in American nuclear testing. Nothing very much was ever publicly said about it. The visit to Jock acted as a catalyst. I began to question, once more, the wisdom and effects of the tests that we had witnessed. I wondered whether there was public interest in the conditions, good and bad, for the servicemen involved.

After Operation DOMINIC I - or BRIGADOON, as it was known for the British forces - there were no further nuclear tests carried out on or around Christmas Island.

In October and November of 1962, the United States carried out nine further tests from Johnson Island (DOMINIC II). These included four high-altitude tests. By 1964, the RAF station on Christmas Island was closed down.

The DOMINIC I tests of 1962 were named as follows:

25	April	ADOBE
27	April	AZTEC
2	May	ARKANSAS
4	May	QUESTA
8	May	YUKON
9	May	MESILLA
11	May	MUSKEGON
12	May	ENCINO
14	May	SWANEE
19	May	CHETCO
25	May	TANANA
27	May	NAMBE
8	June	ALMA
9	June	TRUCKEE
10	June	YESO
12	June	HARLEM
15	June	RINCONADA
17	June	DULCE
19	June	PETIT
22	June	OTOWI
27	June	BIGHORN
30	June	BLUESTONE
8	July	STARFISH
10	July	SUNSET
11	July	PAMLICO

In addition there were two tests in the open ocean: FRIGATE BIRD on 6 May and SWORDFISH on 11 May.

Christmas Island witnessed six previous nuclear tests carried out by the United Kingdom and code named 'Operation Grapple'.

OPERATION GRAPPLE

Grapple X   8 November 1957
Grapple Y 28 April 1958
Grapple Z 22 August 1958
Grapple Z   2 September 1958
Grapple Z 11 September 1958
Grapple Z 23 September 1958

In 1979 the Gilbert and Ellice Islands including Christmas Island, had gained their independence.

According to the Defense Nuclear Agency, Public Affairs Office, in Washington DC, the United States has possession of the film badges issued to servicemen and civilians at that time. This includes those issued to British servicemen. They maintain that the film badge readings were low, with only 3 per cent of the 25,399 badged participants having an exposure greater than 3.0 rem (a rem being a unit of measurement of radiation and the current Federal guideline for permitted dosage being 5.0 rem annual exposure). This department also reports that evidence exists that many of the badges worn by personnel during DOMINIC were defectively sealed. In 1979-1980, there was a revaluation of 1,349, DOMINIC I badges. About half of the badges showed some damage related to light, heat and age. This is purported to have been due to defective wax seals. The Defense Nuclear Agency maintained that there was environmental damage to nearly all the badges which developed a density equivalent of over 0.4 rem (gamma).

It could be said that Britain came off very well, militarily, from the American Operation Dominic tests.

In terms of defence information obtained there was a good return for the use of the island and a handful of men. It may well be that the Polaris weapons developed and tested at that time did help to keep an uneasy peace in Europe as well as the rest of the world. They may have prevented domination under the nuclear jackboot of another country.

It may also be, however, that there is another price which has been paid and is still being paid for past nuclear weapon testing. There have been newspaper articles highlighting problems suffered by some nuclear veterans. Geneticists have indicated that there may be cause for concern and that effects from certain levels of radiation, lower than once thought, may follow through more than one generation. Children born to servicemen after their return have never been monitored. In Britain there has been no check on all participants of British involvement in nuclear weapon testing. It would seem that the British government, at the time of BRIGADOON, left badge-checks of radiation levels on their personnel to be carried out by a foreign power.

Successive British governments have refused to consider any possible connection between nuclear tests and any illness suffered by servicemen. In 1988, The House of Lords gave a veteran of the 1950s nuclear tests permission to sue the government for his illness. He did not survive long enough to see his case through.

In the United States, the Defense Nuclear Agency is currently in the process of identifying each American test participant and evaluating the radiation doses which, according to their records, each received during participation in tests.

Apart from any possible human damage there also remains the question of environmental effects. Is it possible that high altitude testing caused damage? Back down on earth, it is possible some after-effect was certainly felt. A report appearing in *The Mail on Sunday*, dated 5 June 1983, read,

'On Christmas Island in the Pacific - the world's largest coral atoll - the entire bird population of eight species has disappeared off the face of the earth. A concerned coterie of American scientists and bird experts are now on their way there, to find out what happened.'

The team of American scientists eventually blamed the mystery of the birds disappearance on 'El Nino', a combination of unusual weather and tidal conditions. This natural phenomenon occurs every couple of decades in the eastern South Pacific Ocean. Its effects, on fish and birds, are mainly confined to the South American coastal areas. What is so surprising about their conclusion is that Christmas Island is well over 5000 miles away.

In my mind I still see a solitary bird flying against a stark sky made instantly blue from out of the dark night. Its deranged path through the intense light of a man-made day; flying beyond that false dawn to destruction.